Exploring the Fifth Dimension: Parallel Universes, Teleportation and Out-of-Body Travel

Dr. Bruce Goldberg

Published by

Bruce Goldberg, Inc.
4300 Natoma Ave.
Woodland Hills, CA 91364
Telephone: (800) KARMA-4-U or (800) 527-6248
FAX: (818) 704-9189 .
Email: drbg@sbcglobal.net
Web Site:
www.drbrucegoldberg.com

Printed in the United States of America

ISBN 1-57968-012-2

ABOUT THE AUTHOR

Dr. Bruce Goldberg holds a B.A. degree in Biology and Chemistry, is a Doctor of Dental Surgery, and has a Masters degree in Counseling Psychology. He retired from dentistry in 1989, and has concentrated on his hypnotherapy practice in Los Angeles. Dr. Goldberg was trained by the American Society of Clinical Hypnosis in the techniques and clinical applications of hypnosis in 1975.

Dr. Goldberg has interviewed on *Coast to Coast AM, Oprah, Leeza, Joan Rivers, Regis, Tom Snyder, Jerry Springer, Jenny Jones*, and *Montel Williams* shows; by *CNN*, *NBC*, *Fox*, *CBS News*, and many others.

Through lectures, television and radio appearances, and newspaper articles, including interviews in *Time*, *The Los Angeles Times*, *USA Today*, and the *Washington Post*, he has conducted more than 35,000 past-life regressions and future-life progressions since 1974, helping thousands of patients empower themselves through these techniques. His CDs, cassette tapes and DVDs teach people self-hypnosis, and guide them into past and future lives. He gives lectures and seminars on hypnosis, regression and progression therapy, and conscious dying; he is also a consultant to corporations, attorneys, and the local and network media. His first edition of *The Search for Grace*, was made into a television movie by CBS. His third book, the award winning Soul Healing, is a classic on alternative medicine and psychic empowerment. *Past Lives—Future Lives* is Dr. Goldberg's international bestseller and is the first book written on future lives (progression hypnotherapy).

Dr. Goldberg distributes CDs, cassette tapes, and DVDs to teach people self-hypnosis and to guide them into past and future lives and time travel. For information on self-hypnosis tapes, speaking engagements, or private sessions, Dr. Goldberg can be contacted directly by writing to:

Bruce Goldberg, D.D.S., M.S.
4300 Natoma Avenue, Woodland Hills, CA 91364
Telephone: (800) Karma-4.U or (800) 527-6248
Fax: (818) 704-9189
email: drbg@sbcglobal.net
Website: www.drbrucegoldberg.com

Please include a self-addressed, stamped envelope with your letter.

OTHER BOOKS BY
DR. BRUCE GOLDBERG

Past Live, Future Lives
Soul Healing
The Search for Grace: A Documented Case of Murder and Reincarnation
Peaceful Transition: The Art of Conscious Dying and the Liberation of the Soul
New Age Hypnosis
Karmic Capitalism: A Spiritual Approach to Financial Independence
Unleash Your Psychic Powers
Look Younger and Live Longer: Add 25 to 50 Quality Years to Your Life Naturally
Protected by the Light: The Complete Book of Psychic Self Defense
Time Travelers from Our Future: A Fifth Dimension Odyssey
Astral Voyages: Mastering the Art of Interdimensional Travel
Custom Design Your Own Destiny
Self-Hypnosis: Easy Ways to Hypnotize Your Problems Away
Dream Your Problems Away: Heal Yourself While You Sleep
Egypt: An Extraterrestrial and Time Traveler Experiment
Past Lives, Future Lives Revealed
Ascension: The Art of Soul Perfection and the Attainment of Grace

CONTENTS

Acknowledgments

I would like to express my eternal gratitude to George Noory, host of Premiere Radio Network's Coast to Coast AM, for his support and friendship during the many hours we spent on the air discussing the fifth dimension, reincarnation, time travel and other related topics.

I also want to thank George's producer Tom Danheiser, webmasters Lex Lonehood and Shawn La Douceur and all of the Premiere Radio Network people who assist with the show. Lastly, I cannot thank my many patients enough. Without their dynamic experiences and many successes, this book would not have been possible.

Note to the Reader

This book is the result of the professional experiences accumulated by the author since 1974, working individually with more than 15,000 patients. The material included herein is intended to complement, not replace, the advice of your own physician, psychotherapist, or other healthcare professional, whom you should always consult about your circumstances before starting or stopping any medication or any other course of treatment, exercise regimen, or diet.

At times, the masculine pronoun has been used as a convenience. It is intended to indicate both male and female genders where this is applicable. All names and identifying references, except those of celebrities, have been altered to protect the privacy of my patients. All other facts are accurate and have not been altered.

Dr. Bruce Goldberg
Woodland Hills, California

Introduction

The main purpose of this book is to both educate you about the fifth dimension and train you to safely leave the confines of your physical body to explore this fascinating realm.

We will also explore the concept of reincarnation which utilizes the fifth dimension as its mechanism.

Everywhere we look are monstrous problems without evident solutions. Is there no better time to seek the truth? The Theosophists have the axiom, "There is no religion higher than the truth." It is truth that will ultimately save us. Error may often be upon the earthly throne, but it is truth that says the future. If you are unwilling to seek truth and to live in it, you will have no place in the coming New Age.

We need to reach out for new and deep truth boldly and without fear. Exploring the fifth dimension opens up a whole new world for us both figuratively and literally.

Throughout history and especially beginning with the origins of religion and philosophy, man has pondered the notion of life after death. In fact, today the greatest fear we have is that of death - thanatophobia. It is only spiritually evolved souls who have formulated a definite and long-standing belief in some form of life after death, that seem to be relatively free of this phobia. Exploring the fifth dimension will demonstrate the fact that there is no such thing as death, only a change in dimensions. It really doesn't matter how much you enjoy your current life, if you honestly feel this is your one shot at existence, how can you truly be happy or fulfilled?

There are few concepts as controversial and puzzling as that of the fifth dimension. Considering the different concepts of time used in mathematics and physics, or in the theories of relativity and quantum mechanics, to say nothing of the differences between biological time, psychological time, social and historical time, we may doubt the objective existence of the fifth dimension altogether.

In discussing the fifth dimension we will fully explore the concept of simultaneous time and space-time continuum. We will also discuss Parallel Universes, Teleportation and Out-of-Body Travel (OBEs).

I will present many exciting cases from my Los Angeles practice, as well as self-hypnosis exercises, for you to actually experience this wonderful dimension.

Throughout this book the fascinating possibility of time travel will be explored, and theories and evidence illustrating that time travel has been an everyday phenomenon, and that men and women from our own future have come back as time travelers (mistakenly identified as extraterrestrial aliens).

In addition, we will discuss:

- Examples of people who have traveled back, forward and sideways through time and have documented their travels.
- Teleportation cases.
- Hyperspace travel and hyper-universes.
- Out-of-body experiences
- Dreamtime.
- Consciousness and time.
- Past life regression, age progression, future life progression and parallel universes.
- Self-hypnosis exercises that will allow you to travel back or forward in time and custom design your own destiny.
- How to use these time travel principles to attain spiritual growth.
- How time travel through hypnosis to past and future lives demonstrates life after death.

INTRODUCTION

How to Use This Book

This book contains dozens of exercises specifically designed to train you to experience self-hypnosis and to travel through the fifth dimension. It doesn't matter what your background is.

You can accept or reject any of the principles and concepts presented here. Empowerment is vital. I stress that in my Los Angeles hypnotherapy practice and in my personal life as well. If you become rigid and stuck in your views, you become trapped by your beliefs. You are no longer empowered because you are no longer free.

Always use your judgment and free will in trying these exercises. Use the ones you feel comfortable with and ignore the others. These exercises are all perfectly safe and have been tested for more than 35 years. You may create your own exercises from these models.

Read each exercise through to become familiar with it. Use the relaxation techniques given or your own. You may practice alone or with others. I strongly suggest that you make tapes of these exercises. Read the scripts slowly and leave enough space on your tape to experience each part of the procedure. You can order professionally recorded CDs with my voice from my website (www.drbrucegoldberg.com).

Practice once or twice as day, in 15- to 20-minute sessions. In general, it is considered more efficient to practice in the morning, as it may provide a relaxing start for the entire day. The more specific and realistic your schedule, the better the chances that you will succeed.

You should choose a part of your day when you are at your best. If you wait to practice until long after you get home from a hard day at work you might only practice going to sleep. Self-hypnosis is more efficient if practiced when you are reasonably alert.

If you wake up alert and rested first thing in the morning, practice then, before getting out of bed. Take into account whether or not you will be disturbed by spouse, lover, kids, pets, and so forth. Choose a time when you are not likely to be interrupted. Other popular times are before lunch or dinner.

Four components of successful self-hypnosis are:

- A quiet environment.
- A mental device.
- A passive attitude.
- A comfortable position.

When you enter into a self-hypnotic trance, you will observe the following:

- A positive mood (tranquility, peace of mind).
- An experience of unity or oneness with the environment.
- An inability to describe the experience in words.
- An alteration in time/space relationships.
- An enhanced sense of reality and meaning.

If you experience difficulty with an exercise, do not become frustrated. Some techniques are quite advanced and you may not be ready for all of them. Return to the ones you could not successfully master at another time.

Practice these trance states when you have time and are relaxed. Be patient. It takes time to master trance states and to become accustomed to this new and wonderful world. No one way is the right way to experience a trance. Your body may feel light, or it may feel heavy; you may feel as if you are dreaming; your eyelids may flutter; or your body can become cooler or warmer. All these possible responses are perfectly safe.

Because you will be unfamiliar with the techniques at first, your initial practice sessions should run as long as you need. As you become more proficient, you will be able to shorten these sessions. Some days nothing may seem to work. Try not to become discouraged. Remember that other days will be more fruitful. Always work at your own pace.

Dr. Goldberg's website www.drbrucebgoldberg.com)
has New Age music only CDs, as well as
professionally recorded CDs, for many of the
exercises presented in this book.

To use this book effectively, you must be prepared to take control of your own self-analysis, self-exploration, and self-discovery. Be prepared to chart your own course of psychic empowerment, and solve the mystery that is yourself.

CHAPTER 1

IN SEARCH OF THE TRUTH

Indian philosophy is often referred to by metaphysicians in an attempt to illustrate a truth. One of my favorite stories from the East concerns a young student and an old yogi, his teacher. One day while both were walking along the Ganges river, the young student asked his teacher, "Master, what must I do and feel in order to progress in my knowledge of the truth and of God?"

The yogi suddenly seized the young man and took him to the river. There the old man forcibly held the student's head under the water. The youth began to struggle and finally the teacher let him breathe again. The yogi is reported to have uttered, "Son, when you yearn for truth as much as your lungs just gasped for air, then come to me and I shall be able to teach you!"

Few of us have the necessary intensity of desire for truth. Most people simply lack the discipline and the inner thirst for the knowledge that will ultimately lead them to a higher conscious mind realization of spiritual growth and the ultimate truth. Fortunately, the numbers of potential initiates and empowered souls is growing.

As Socrates said, "truth, like virtue, is its own reward." Truth, wisdom and spiritual growth represent the highest goals of the mind. The original sin is ignorance, according to the Easterners. Wisdom, virtual and spiritual growth result from the manifestation of the perfect component of our soul known as the Higher Self.

I can think of no greater purpose than of seeking the ultimate truth. For with this endeavor will come wisdom and spiritual growth. This is the true reason why we are all here. It is not our purpose merely to earn money, reproduce or do our civic duty. These responsibilities have their place on the earth plane, but what about our soul?

If you cannot answer the question why you are here other than with simple material responsibilities, you have missed the point. Your life will, in reality, not mean very much. You will live in vain and merely become part of the food chain. However, if you are open to an in depth, no holds barred exploration of truth, then read on. This book will present a plethora of "truths" that will help you to move in the right direction.

There is temptation in today's world to be a materialist. The technological toys and comfort devices lull most of us into a materialistic form of mass hypnosis. The world of the five senses constitutes the entire universe, according to the materialist. Nothing else is real. Death is final and nothing exists after physical death.

If that were true, this book would be a complete waste of time. Karl Marx would be proven correct when he said religion was "the opium of the masses."

Materialists need artificial stimulation. They resort to drugs, sex, power and money, to name a few. Their reason is simple, they are miserable. I also place the skeptic in this category. A truly fulfilled and empowered person does not need anything or anyone. They may desire or want things, but they do not have to have it.

Idealists have the opposite view. They acknowledge the existence of the material world, but to them this world is not real. Matter is reduced to energy via Einstein's famous equation E MC^2. A further link in the truth chain is added in that all energy proceeds from mind or consciousness. The last link in this chain is the God energy that creates consciousness in the first place.

We live in a world full of illusions in which our five senses seduce and deceive us every day. Metaphysics is the study of spiritual growth and consciousness. Its ultimate goal is to raise consciousness to God. But even the mystics warns us that all teachings and metaphysical writings must be regarded as fingers pointing to the moon rather than as the moon itself.

Over 2,500 years ago a man in northern India finally found his ultimate truth. He had been searching for this truth for many lifetimes. One day he sat under a Bodhi tree and decided not to get up until he had found the truth.

By the next morning, this man was rewarded for his patience, discipline and concentration and achieved enlightenment. The Indian scriptures report that at that sacred moment the earth itself shuddered, as if "drunk with bliss." These writings further aver, "No one anywhere was angry, ill, or sad; no one did evil, none was proud, the world became quite quiet, as though it had reached full perfection."

In case you haven't guessed, this man became known to the world as the Buddha. The Vietnamese master Thich Nhat Hanh's description of Buddha's enlightenment is as follows:

> Gautama felt as though a prison which had confined him for thousands of lifetimes had broken open. Ignorance had been the jail keeper. Because of ignorance, his mind had been obscured, just like the moon and stars hidden by the storm clouds. Clouded by endless waves of deluded thoughts, the mind had falsely divided reality into subject and object, self and others, existence and non-existence, birth and death, and from these discriminations arose wrong views-the prisons of feelings, craving, grasping, and becoming. The suffering of birth, old age, sickness, and death only made the prison walls thicker. The only thing to do was to seize the jail keeper and see his true face. The jail keeper was

ignorance. . . Once the jail keeper was gone, the jail would disappear and never be rebuilt again.[1]

The distinction between truth and reality is one between philosophy and life. Truth, in its scientific and philosophic sense, is always abstract. All of its determinations are merely concept-forms. The main distinction between truth and reality is that, whereas in reality we are concerned with the alogical as well as with the logical, in truth we are dealing, at least primarily, with the logical alone. Reality places its first priority on logic. Truth, on the other hand, regards logic as secondary, as reflected by the mind. Truth can never be identical with reality. Truth is always abstract as being concerned essentially with logical notions, whereas reality is concrete; it represents the synthetic union of the alogical and the logical.

In truth reality is always transformed. The perception of the real object disappears, and is replaced by a thought-form-a more or less arbitrary symbol of itself.

This symbol works all very well up to a certain point for practical purposes, but beyond that point it breaks down, and we get into contradictions, or impossibilities of thought.

For example, consider the liar's paradox. Assume you were in Ancient Greece in the company of an individual from Sparta. The man from Sparta declares, "All Spartans are liars." Is this person telling the truth, or is he lying?

If he is telling the truth, then all Spartans are liars, so he is also lying-that's a contradiction. On the other hand, if he is lying, then all Spartans are not liars, and he may very well be telling the truth. This presents another contradiction.

The ultimate truth stands for the most complete expression of those determinations of consciousness we term reality. Truth means the expression in the forms of reflective thought, the most perfect expression of the reality of a given plane of consciousness.

A truth is only absolute for its own plane and for those below it. Otherwise, by its very nature it becomes, that is, it evolves from within itself, a higher truth, in respect of which it becomes itself falsehood. The highest truth would be identical with the ultimate truth, but below or within this all comprehensive aspect we find infinite gradations of relative truth.

Every department of knowledge has its special truth. The truth of physics is not precisely the truth of chemistry. The truth of chemistry is just as little the truth of physiology. The truth of physiology again differs from the truth of social science. Truth, in this scientific sense, coincides with the system of laws of a given science. The confusion between these relative truths of science , and their misapplication, have often been recognized as a source of fallacy.

The ultimate reality is viewed as the highest expression of reality.   It is the summation of each and every individual unconsciousness, but it is only completely understood from the perspective of a supreme or all inclusive consciousness. Reality is always a perfection, in the sense, whether relative or absolute.

The man-in-the-street calls the outer world-the content of his waking perceptive consciousness, working through the forms of space and time-reality. In doing so he confines the world to the plane of consciousness that is of most obvious importance (to himself) for everyday life and its practical concerns. This common-sense reality is also a perfection and completion, the perfection and completion of the sensations and the bare thought-forms of which it is constructed, and which disclose themselves to metaphysical analysis.

Man cannot live without faith and a positive anticipation of the future. But doors are closing in the material world; the frontier is gone , and the concept, to some, of an ever-expanding and prospering America is being badly shaken. The Vietnam, and even the short Persian Gulf wars, disillusioned us with the military as a solution to our problems. Our political life is not doing very well at the moment, and the prospect of grave political convulsions lies before us. Economics cannot save us, and on every side are challenges to the existing system. The United Nations is seen as an impotent debating society, ham-stringing America in no-win wars. Sociology is not the answer, nor are the inept social sciences.

CHAPTER 1

Psychology and psychiatry have their uses, but they do not have the strength nor consensus to save us from our plight.

The New Age vibrations are getting stronger every year, and I feel them beating at the doors of my awareness. We will soon behold the light of the New Age and there will be fond rejoicing. There will be the revelation of the ultimate truth.

With this background, we can now begin our journey in search of the ultimate truth and the wonders of the fifth dimension.

---

[1]   Thich Nhat Hanh, *Old Path, White Clouds*, Parallax Press, Berkeley, CA 1991, p. 121.

CHAPTER 2

The Fifth Dimension

Wouldn't it be great to just think about flying like Superman, or running at incredible speeds mimicking the Flash? Our physical dimension has certain physical laws which prohibit such action, but on the fifth dimension all things are possible.

To comprehend the fifth dimension, we must define the first four dimensions of our universe. Length, width and depth (height) represent the first three dimensions. We are able to observe these with our two eyes. Time is viewed as the fourth dimension. In reality time is the fourth dimension of the space-time continuum. We cannot "see" time. Anything beyond time is considered the fifth dimension.

To view this fifth dimension we must utilize our "third , eye," or 6th chakra. This requires us to leave our physical body and enter into hyperspace, since our physical eyes were not designed to see beyond three dimensions.

The new physics (quantum physics or quantum mechanics) demonstrates the existence of parallel universes. Each of these parallel universes, along with other dimensions such as the astral, causal, mental, etheric and soul plane, lie in hyperspace at different frequencies and represent the fifth dimension.

The fifth dimension consists of a basic framework of permanent structures. These fixed areas exist without our efforts and cannot be altered by our consciousness. No form created by us may be allowed to enter these specially designated areas. Reality here is organized by a completely different set of laws.

For example, you may find yourself totally immersed in tones and hues of energy and feeling. You may be deeply moved by waves of emotions, leaving no visual impression whatsoever. Strange and alluring music of unearthly character may engulf you.

Colors may be felt and sounds could very well be seen in certain unconventional regions of the dream world. This may seem alien to you, but it is important to get what you can from this exposure. In time our subconscious may choose to inform us what this all meant in our quest for spiritual growth.

Another unusual, yet beautiful, experience in this realm is a merging with our Higher Self. This exposure is characterized by feelings of exaltation and bliss. You may now see the workings of reality more clearly than ever before. A feeling of greater purpose will be one result of this union.

When we travel to the fifth dimension objects are viewed in unusual ways. For example:

- You can remove an object from an enclosed container without penetrating its walls. Teleportation is possible in that an object can be made to dematerialize from one location and rematerialize to another spot.

- A flexible sphere can be turned inside out without tearing it.

- You do not have to break the links of a chain to separate it.

- It is possible to untie a knot in a rope without moving the ends of it.

When we travel through hyperspace into the fifth dimension a vast array of colors and sounds may be evident. If you think back to the ending of the movie *2001: A Space Odyssey*, you may be able to relate to this effect.

Here are some commonly observed phenomena in the fifth dimension:

- Small stars, triangular ships and other geometrically shaped objects may be observed in the sky.

- A glowing light surrounds both people and objects. People may appear as pulsating lights of varying Intensities or possess alien or human-like bodies.

- The sky may appear as a blue, green or purple swirling mist.

- The only thing that may confine a fifth dimensional object or being are magnetic fields and thought patterns.

- Rooms appear as swirling lights and energy points, with black voids functioning as entry and exit points.

- Sudden flashes of color, moving through a tunnel and an assortment of unusual sounds are commonly noted.

- Although there are fixed components of the fifth dimension, your mind can create most anything it wants to add to it by merely thinking it.

- Telepathy, telekinesis, teleportation, precognition and other psychic skills are the norm.

- Precipitation is observed as glowing snowflakes or multicolored, shiny raindrops. The climate, however, is almost always spring or summer-like.

- For the most part, fifth dimension worlds are well-organized, clean, peaceful and serene. The one exception is the lower astral plane, where we find dysfunctional beings and an occasional demon.

- Fifth dimensional bodies do not require food or sex. The sex that is found there is one of an energy transfer.

- Pregnancy is unknown on the fifth dimension. Its inhabitants can materialize babies and young children if they so desire.

- An injured fifth dimension body is instantly healed through the use of our mind. Sleep is not necessary.

- We can view our akashic records and learn our true karmic purpose on any of these other dimensions.

- Time travelers spend much of their time in the fifth dimension.
- In summary, we can describe the fifth dimension as having the following characteristics:

- Each world is composed of energy and matter representing a higher frequency vibrational rate (FVR) than the physical plane.

- Each plane functions independently of each other, due to this difference in the FVR.

- Landscapes, buildings and most people appear earth-like. All communication is by telepathy.

- There are no physical laws per se on the fifth dimension. Although gravity does not exist, we can choose to walk on the ground. We may also fly or float to our destination.

- Only a very small percentage of fifth dimension beings resemble cartoon characters or aliens. These are mostly confined to the lower astral plane.

- The language that is spoken on the fifth dimension is whatever your native language is on the physical plane and communication is by telepathy.

Hypnosis: What is it?

Hypnosis is the technique we will use to explore the fifth dimension. All forms of daydreaming are natural levels of hypnosis. They are characterized by focused concentration, relaxation, lack of movement, and an increase in sensory reception. Other examples of natural day-to-day hypnosis are reading a book, watching television, doing detailed work for extended periods of time, and performing any enjoyable task where time appears to pass quickly.

We experience approximately four hours of daydreams or natural hypnotic states during our waking day. Our nighttime dreams are another form of hypnosis usually occurring during the REM (rapid eye movement) cycle of sleep. We dream for approximately three hours every night.

Projecting this out, we experience seven hours of natural hypnosis during every twenty-four-hour day cycle-approximately 2,500 hours in a year! A forty-year-old reader of this book would have spent an average of 100,000 hours in natural hypnosis throughout his or her life. That is equivalent to doing for eight uninterrupted hours a day, five days a week, fifty weeks per year for fifty years, some menial task that you have completed hundreds of times. Remember, this hypothetical reader is only forty years old!

Hypnosis is induced in our daily lives by repetitive commercials, a good orator, advertising propaganda, and evangelistic appeals. We set aside our *conscious mind proper* (beta brain wave level on the electroencephalograph) and establish direct communication with our *subconscious mind* (alpha brain wave).

There are two other brain waves, theta and delta, that represent light and deep sleep respectively, but they do not concern us in our discussion of hypnosis. Modern medicine has established the fact that hypnosis is not a sleep state.

Since a medium-level hypnotic trance is characterized by amnesia and deep levels of relaxation, it is not difficult to see how the layperson could make this erroneous association. Remember that the idea of hypnosis being a sleep state was implanted by stage hypnotists, novelists, and Hollywood.

The conscious mind proper is our ego. Easily distracted, the conscious mind's concentration rate is only twenty-five percent efficient. This state of mind analyzes and criticizes everything, and dies when the physical body dies. We spend about twelve hours a day in our conscious mind-proper state.

The subconscious or alpha state is most important to our understanding of hypnosis. Its concentration efficiency is nearly perfect at a minimum of ninety-five percent. We enter this state just before going to sleep and upon arising, as well as in periods of daydreaming, meditation, yoga, and similar mind states. As you can see, hypnosis (alpha) is not a sleep state, but a *natural* and efficient waking state of mind.

Hypnosis is simply a way of relaxing and setting aside the conscious mind proper, while at the same time activating the subconscious mind so that suggestions can be made directly, enabling the subject to act on these suggestions with greater ease and efficiency.

The term "heterohypnosis" is used to describe the induction of a subject into a hypnotic trance by another person (the hypnotist). If one does this to him- or herself, we refer to this as self-hypnosis or autohypnosis.

Most hypnosis is self-hypnosis. The hypnotist does not project hypnosis onto the subject. The subject decides when to accept this hypnotic state. The "gift" of hypnosis always lies with the subject, not the hypnotist. The hypnotist may set the stage and create an appropriate environment, but he or she cannot force the hypnotic state on the subject.

The hypnotic trance state will have certain basic characteristics. These are:

1. A generalized feeling of relaxation.

2. A sense of time moving quickly. You will actually have no idea how much real time elapsed.

3. Focused concentration.

4. A lack of movement in your body.

5. Your eyes may move back and forth (rapid eye movement, or REM).

In deeper levels of hypnosis (as well as in all dream states), it is possible to experience an OBE. When you have an OBE, you are in a truly altered state of consciousness. In this state of deeper trance, you may observe the following features:

- **Alterations in thinking.** Subjective interruptions in memory, judgment, attention, and concentration characterize this feature.

- **Sense of the ineffable.** People who experience an ASC (altered state of consciousness) appear unable to communicate the essence of their experience to someone who has not had one. Amnesia is also noted.

- **Disturbed time sense.** Common to this are subjective feelings of time coming to a standstill, feelings of timelessness, and the slowing or acceleration of time.

- **Feelings of rejuvenation.** A new sense of hope, joy, and purpose is exhibited by the experiencer.

- **Change in meaning or significance.** Feelings of profound insight, illumination, and truth are frequently observed in ASC.

- **Changes in emotional expression.** Displays of more intense and primitive emotional expressions that are sudden and unexpected. Emotional detachment may also be exhibited at this time.

- **Body image change.** A sense of depersonalization, derealization, and a loss of boundaries between self and others or the universe are observed. These encounters can be called "expansion of consciousness," or feelings of "oneness" in a mystical or religious setting. Not only may various parts of the body appear or feel shrunken, enlarged, distorted, heavy, weightless, disconnected, strange or funny, but spontaneous experiences of dizziness, blurring of vision, weakness, numbness, tingling, and analgesia are likewise encountered.

In reference to using self-hypnosis for your positive programming there are certain principles you should understand to relieve any fear about this technique:

1. The best hypnotic subjects are people who are imaginative and intelligent. The more determined you are to attain a goal, the greater your chances of success.

2. You cannot be forced to do anything as a result of hypnosis that you would not normally do.

3. Hypnotic programming works by repeated exposure. Eventually when you raise the quality of your soul's

energy, you will establish a new spiritual as well as emotional foundation, and your programming becomes a permanent part of your awareness.

4. You will remember everything that you experience during a trance, unless you are a very deep-level subject.

5. After a self-hypnotic experience, you will awaken feeling more at peace, relaxed, and cleansed (both emotionally and spiritually) than you felt prior to this experience. If you practice this technique at bedtime, you will probably fall asleep and guide your dream level based on the suggestions you gave yourself.

Our subconscious mind is like a computer that stores everything we observe by our five senses. This also includes past and future life data, since the subconscious (soul) reincarnates and can never be destroyed. Many of us have been misprogrammed to fear that hypnosis is either dangerous or a form of mind control.

Fears and fallacies about hypnosis are commonly reported by my patients. Here is how I respond to these concerns:

*   **The fallacy of mind control.** I have already pointed out that it is the subject, not the hypnotist, that determines whether the hypnotic state is to occur.

*   **The fear of revealing secrets in trance.** The subject always maintains this control. If I ask a subject to answer a question about their past or future life experience, they can answer or not answer my query at their discretion. The hypnotist cannot force the subject to answer.

*   **The fear of not remembering suggestions after the trance ends.** Only very deep level subjects will experience this type of amnesia. The hypnotist can eliminate this

problem by giving an appropriate suggestion for the subject to remember everything when the trance ends.

- **The fear of not being able to leave the hypnotized state.** Hypnosis is a natural state of mind. We all come out of this state when we are ready. All of my scripts include wakening instructions.

- **The fear of being trapped in a past or future life.** I have conducted more than 35,000 past life regressions and future life progressions on more than 15,000 individual patients since 1974, and I have never had this problem.

A Self-Hypnosis Exercise

The following is an exercise for self-hypnosis that I developed in my early years in private practice. You may find it useful to listen to a recording of yourself reading this script.

Stage 1

Go into a room and close the door to shut out distracting sounds. Lie down on a bed or couch and relax as best you can for from two to five minutes. The mind and body both will tend to relax as you lay inert, and this passive state will open a door into the subconscious mind. As you lie quietly, close your eyes and think of a warm, relaxing feeling.

Focus all your attention on the muscles in the toes of both of your feet. Imagine this warm, relaxing feeling spreading and surrounding the muscles of the toes of both feet, moving to the backs of both feet and to the heels and ankles. Now imagine this warm feeling moving up through the calf muscles of both legs to the

kneecap and into the thigh muscles meeting at the hip bone.

The warm, relaxing feeling is moving up the backbone to the middle of the back, surrounding the shoulder blades and moving into the back of the neck.

The warm, relaxing feeling is now moving into the fingers of both hands, just like it did with the toes. This feeling now spreads into the backs of both hands, palms, wrists, forearms, elbows, shoulders and neck, relaxing each and every muscle along its path.

The warm, relaxing feeling now moves into the intestines, stomach, chest, and neck muscles.

This warm, relaxing feeling moves into the back of the head, scalp, and all the way to the forehead. Now, the facial muscles are relaxed; now the eyes (which are closed), bridge of the nose, jaws (the teeth are separated), chin, ear lobes, and neck. Now each and every muscle in the entire body is so completely relaxed.

When you actually develop a generalized, relaxed feeling throughout your body or a heaviness in your arms or legs, you have reached the light stages of hypnosis. Continue with the exercise for several days, then progress to the second stage, which is more advanced. The instructions are a mental dialogue that you will have with yourself. Read it over two or three times and absorb the general idea rather than trying to remember it word for word, or as an alternative, tape record yourself reading it aloud.

CHAPTER 2

Stage 2

To go deeper into hypnosis is just about everybody's chief concern. This can be accomplished in a number of ways. One of the more common is to imagine a very pleasant and soothing scene, such as a green valley that you are looking down into from a mountain top, and watching a lazy brook meander its way through the valley, relaxing you more and more as you watch its slow movements. Another way is to imagine yourself descending a flight of stairs very slowly, while thinking to yourself as you wind down the ancient stone stairwell that you are going deeper and deeper and deeper with each step. The following script is an example of deepening the hypnotic trance state:

I want you to imagine that you are standing on the fifth floor of a large department store...and that you are just stepping into the elevator to descend to street level. And as you go down and as the elevator door opens and closes as you arrive at each floor... you will become more and more deeply relaxed... and your sleep will become deeper and deeper.

The doors are closing now...and you are beginning to sink slowly downward.

The elevator stops at the fourth floor...several people get out...two more get in...the doors close again...and already you are becoming more and more deeply relaxed...more and more deeply asleep.

And as you sink to the third floor...and stop, while the doors open and close again... you are relaxing more and more...and your sleep is becoming deeper and deeper.

You slowly sink down to the second floor...one or two people get out and several get in...and as they do so...you are feeling much more deeply relaxed... much more deeply asleep.

Down once again to the first floor...the doors open and close...but nobody gets out or in. Already you have become still more deeply relaxed...and your sleep still deeper and deeper. Deeper and deeper asleep...deeper and deeper asleep.

Down further and further... until the elevator stops at last at street level. The doors open...and everybody gets out. But you do not get out. You decide to go still deeper...and descend to the basement.

The elevator doors close again...and down you go...down and down...deeper and deeper...and as you arrive at the basement...you are feeling twice as deeply and comfortably relaxed...twice as deeply asleep.

As you develop skill with your own mind, you will be able to go into hypnosis much more quickly and even surroundings that used to be too distracting for you to handle will now become tolerable for practicing self-hypnosis.

With subsequent hypnotic sessions, you will easily learn how to develop these relaxed states. The more exposure you receive, the easier and better it will be for you.

Components of the Fifth Dimension

In order to understand the fifth dimension, we need to describe its various components.

The Lower Five Planes

1. **The earth plane or physical plane.** This is the plane that we function in now. The body is most material or physical at this level. The greatest amount of karma can be erased or added on at this level. This is by far the most difficult level.

2. **The astral plane.** The body is less material here. This is where the subconscious, or soul, goes immediately following death or crossing over. Ghosts are examples of astral bodies.

3. **The causal plane.** The body is even less material at this level. The akashic records are kept here. This is where a medium projects him or herself when he or she reads your past or future.

4. **The mental plane.** This is the plane of pure intellect.

5. **The etheric plane.** The body is least material at this level. On this plane, truth and beauty are the ultimate values.

It is the thoughts and actions of the soul that determine the amount of time spent on these lower planes. Each of these planes is noted for providing an environment to learn certain spiritual lessons. For example, truth is associated with the etheric plane, while intellectual tasks are deferred to the mental plane. The earth plane represents the plane of greatest elimination or addition to our karmic debts.

The Soul Plane

This plane (plane 6) is an intermediary or "demilitarized zone" between the lower planes and higher planes. This is where the Higher Self spends most of its time, and it is here that a soul chooses its next lifetime. The white light, as often described by near-death experiencers, is actually the Higher Self, which escorts the soul to the soul plane. Masters and Guides and departed loved ones may also be in attendance at this location. Telepathy is the mode of communication and there are no secrets. Any entity now can literally read your mind. so truth in its pure form is evident.

You will be shown fragments of your most recent incarnation here along with several other of your past lives and future life options. The Masters and Guides and your Higher Self will often advise, but it will always your choice as to your next life. The soul always has free will. Until your soul has learned all of its karmic lessons and is perfect, you must reincarnate on the lower planes. Life on these other planes isn't very different from that on the earth plane. People get married, have children, divorce, love, hate, etc. on all of the lower planes

Our karmic cycle, according to the plane concept, is worked out on five lower planes. Our soul is characterized by a level of awareness or vibrational rate. You must raise the quality of your vibrational rate to ascend to a higher plane. Each successive plane requires a higher vibrational rate. The entity will seek the plane that best fits its level.

The Seven Higher Planes

You may choose any of the lower five planes to work out your karma, but as long as you have a karmic cycle you cannot enter the seven higher planes - your vibrational rate would be too low to permit it.

These seven higher planes reach their apex with the God or nameless plane (Number 13). The essence - our true nature - resides on the God plane. It is our SOURCE, the ONE, ALL THAT IS, and many other descriptive names-this is the heaven or nirvana we have come to know by our religious training.

The quality of your spiritual growth as manifested by your souls frequency vibrational rate determines which plane you are able to enter. Your thoughts and actions control this quality. If your vibrational rate qualifies you for the tenth plane, then you cannot enter any higher plane until this rate is increased appropriately.

This concept does not include a Hell. Hell is simply the negative lives you live on the earth plane. There is, however, a heaven or nirvana. It is part of your empowerment to control your thoughts and actions so that you may once again join with God.

The plane concept can best be illustrated by the diagram on the previous page (Fig. 1). From this diagram of the cycle of birth and death, you can see that it is no picnic. The most desirable solution is to perfect the soul as quickly as possible and ascend into the higher planes. Another option is to remain on as a Master or Guide and assist other souls in their ascension. The fastest route to this perfect state is conscious dying.

The energies of the universe, both physical and nonphysical, are at our disposal. We either use them correctly, or misuse and abuse them. Sometimes we do not use them at all because we do not know how.

To some extent we have learned how to use physical energies. We have developed sciences and technologies of physical energy by which we have created some conveniences and comforts in our physical lives. We have also misused and abused these energies, resulting in the pollution of our environment, the poisoning of our bloodstream, and the ever-present threat of nuclear destruction.

Our ignorance is manifested in the energy of thought. We deal with it only as an electro-chemical reaction in the brain cells. The energy of consciousness is dealt with in a similar way.

	God or Nameless	*Plane 13*
		Plane 12
Seven		Plane 11
Higher		Plane 10
Planes		Plane 9
		Plane 8
		Plane 7
	Soul Plane	*Plane 6*
Karmic	Etheric	Plane 5
Cycle —	Mental	Plane 4
Five	Causal	Plane 3—*Akashic Records*
Lower	Astral	Plane 2
Planes	Earth	Plane 1—*You Are Here*

Figure 1
The Progression of the 13 Planes

Dream World

Dreams are far more than just a symbolic representation of communication from your subconscious. Our subconscious never really sleeps, and when our physical body is unconscious and resting, our soul is traveling to other dimensions under the guidance of our Higher Self and Spiritual Masters. The memories of fragments of this tutoring appear as a dream.

Dreams are as valid and relevant to our lives as our waking state. The only real difference is that our dreams take place on a different plane of existence. This is why it is so difficult to understand and decode our dreams based on conventional paradigms.

The world of dreams is quite different from the physical realm we label as our reality. The medieval alchemists called that dimension the astral plane, and this world is equivalent to the Christian concept of purgatory, the bardo of the Tibetans, and the Greek underworld of Hades. This astral plane is a real world, with inhabitants, houses, objects, and other structures.

This realm of illusion is partially created by our emotions and imagination. The astral plane is reportedly considerably larger than our physical world. Every object in the material world has an astral counterpart composed of astral matter.

23

CHAPTER 2

What we have referred to as the fifth dimension is actually the dream world of the astral plane, where all past, present, and future events occur simultaneously. Time does not exist there as we have come to know it. Actions that take several hours on our world occur "in the twinkling of an eye" in the dream universe.

Don't let the illusion of the physical world fool you. We can only perceive what our five senses can detect, unless we have highly developed psychic abilities. There are several forms of energy outside the normal sense detection spectrum. Ultraviolet rays, radio waves, rays, and cosmic radiation are among those energies we cannot detect without the aid of sophisticated scientific instruments.

Dreams exist in an environment that is also composed of energy. This energy is of a different order from that which we are able to measure physically. Our scientific instruments can't portray this except for the alpha brain waves registered on an electroencephalograph (EEG). We can't see our dreams on a television monitor or capture them in a test tube. Yet those things called dreams most certainly do exist.

Our dream world is quite real. I cannot offer hard scientific evidence to support my hypothesis. Just as science cannot absolutely prove that the physical world is real, we have not found a way to measure the existence of the world of dreams. Reality is an elusive concept and it is hard to quantify and define.

One of the great benefits of dreaming is a total freedom to create whatever we wish. This dream environment changes shape according to the will and imagination of the dreamer. This is due to the energy structure and less rigid nature of its environment. This is why the world of dreams is so subjective.

In discussing the dream world we must always keep in mind that entering this dimension frees us from the limitations of the Earth plane and the laws of space and time. This etheric or unreal environment is characterized by shadowy figures moving through a fog-like mist. This environment may take the appearance of heaven, with vivid colors and a brilliant white or gold light.

The dream body that we possess in this environment is composed of a less material substance known as astral matter. This astral body is weightless, but possesses very acute perceptive abilities, especially toward bright, vivid colors, and sound. It appears to sparkle and resembles our physical body in size and shape. It appears somewhat transparent, yet filled with many tiny white stars. Whatever we call it, this dream body is the home of the chakras or energy centers described by the yogis.

The dream body is subject to the laws of the dream environment or the astral plane. Positive dreams take place in the upper astral plane, while nightmares are remnants of trips to the lower astral plane. These two realms correspond with the Upper World and Lower World of the shamans.

We can compare these two aspects of the astral plane as follows:

Lower Astral Plane	**Upper Astral Plane**
1. Feelings of confusion and bewilderment.	1. Feeling alert, secure, peaceful and happy.
2. Misty or foggy environment.	2. Earth-like and beautiful environment.
3. The presence of bizarre and evil inhabitants.	3. The presence of human inhabitants
4. No possibility of spiritual growth.	4. Unlimited spiritual growth.

It is not difficult to see how the concepts of heaven and hell evolved from ancient dream voyagers to the astral plane. Since our dream body is not subject to our physical plane, we cannot be injured regardless of what takes place on the dream dimension. This nonphysical body is affected by nonphysical stimuli and interacts with nonphysical beings and objects.

As we create this vast panorama, we may experience only a certain facet of it that we care to explore. This can result in our failing to perceive some things that are clearly within the range of our perceptions. Sometimes we just can't see the forest for the trees.

We may also sense the presence of departed souls. The astral body of people undergoing near-death experiences and simple astral projection may also be encountered in dream world.

The distance our dream body travels is at the speed of light and is directly proportional to the desire and will of the astral body. All the dream body has to do is think of a location, and it arrives there in an instant.

Lucid Dreaming

When you are aware that you are dreaming during a dream, this is referred to as a lucid dream. This cognitive awareness can range from a thought, "This must be a dream," to a comprehensive freedom of consciousness and of all restrictions of time and space.

One of the great advantages of lucid dreaming is that anything is possible. You can design any scenario you please. Imagine the pleasure and enjoyment potential of the following possibilities:

- Make love with any celebrity or other desirable person anywhere in the world or from history.

- Communicate with departed loved ones.

- Solve any current or future problem.

- Brainstorm creative ideas.

- Fly anywhere in the universe.

- Experience any type of positive emotion or existential paradigm.

To become a lucid dreamer, you must learn the technique of becoming conscious during your dreams. This is not commonly encountered by most of us. When our dreams are routine and dull, we ignore them. Dreams that become too bizarre or fearful overwhelm us and make it impossible to assimilate the dream figure.

The ideal is to establish a healthy balance in your dreams in which you both interact with your dream players in exciting scenarios and still retain your awareness that it is still a dream.

By not preprogramming the entire plot, the lucid dream retains its characteristic of a "stimulating adventure," so the element of surprise is still a component of the dream. You are aware that you can change, stop, and shape negative events to convert them into positive resolutions.

Lucid dreaming requires a constant state of awareness. This not so easy, as your mind will oscillate in and out of awareness. One simple method to assure lucidity is to repeatedly say to yourself, "I am dreaming, and anything is possible." Failing to do this results in conversion of a lucid dream into an ordinary dream. This is uncontrolled, and none of the empowerment we will discuss with lucid dreaming approaches is now possible.

The other extreme may also nullify your lucid dream. If you become too aware during the dream state, you will awaken. As with many therapeutic techniques, a delicate balance must be established. The significance here is that you are responsible for this balance, not a therapist. This further fosters independence and empowerment.

To develop the ability to experience lucid dreaming, the initial step is to recognize when you are in a *prelucid* state. A prelucid dream is characterized by your suspecting that you are dreaming. You are not fully aware that you are dreaming at this time. An expression common to this phase is, "Am I dreaming?" or, "Is this real?"

Reality testing is the mechanism used to determine both prelucid states and lucid dreaming. It is imperative that you test the reality of your experience during the actual dream. Becoming more aware of these prelucid states makes it easier to transform the dream into a true lucid one.

False awakenings are common during lucid dreams. If you feel you have awakened during your dream, but soon realize that this is still a dream (due to the results of your reality testing), you are experiencing a false awakening. These phenomena are known to occur in prelucid dreams also.

Here is a simple technique to induce a lucid dream:

1. **At some time in the early morning when you have awakened spontaneously from a dream, quickly go over every detail of the dream in your mind and repeat the process several times until you have completely memorized the dream.**

2. **While you are still lying in bed, repeat to yourself several times, "Next time I'm dreaming, I want to remember to recognize that I'm dreaming."**

3. **After repeating this phrase, picture yourself back in the dream you just finished dreaming, only imagining that this time you realize that you are dreaming.**

4. **Keep the visualization in your mind until it is clearly fixed or you fall back to sleep.**

Additional methods to create lucid dreams or transform an ordinary dream into a lucid one are presented by these simple approaches:

- Recognize the discrepancies in your dreams. Prepare yourself by giving your subconscious directions to critically analyze the data it receives during this imagery.

Identify any irregularity and immediately focus on the unreality of this dream.

- Suggest you have a nightmare and program yourself to awaken from it during a specific incident. By awaken I mean a false awakening so that your dream environment will become peaceful and you will continue in this dream, now fully aware that you are dreaming.

- Program yourself to have a flying dream. Flying dreams are far more characteristic of lucid dreams than they are of regular dreams. This type of suggestion works rather quickly and well.

- To summarize how we can use lucid dreaming to dream our problems away, consider the following:

- Lucid dreaming is maintaining a conscious awareness that you are dreaming during a dream. It is more difficult than ordinary dreaming, but anyone can master this technique.

- Practicing skills in lucid dreams improves your performance of them in your waking state.

- Use reality testing to check on prelucid states, and convert these to true lucid dreams.

- Repeat to yourself, "This is only a dream and I can't be harmed," to establish and maintain lucidity.

- Lucid dreams may be induced by:
  Becoming so scared that you realize you are dreaming.
  Recognizing dreamlike qualities, unusual occurrences, and incongruities in your dream.

Developing a critical approach during your dream.

The hours of 5 a.m. to 8 a.m. are the easiest to induce lucid dreams for most people.

Lucid dreams are usually realistic, except for flying. Specific recent details may be distorted.

Use reality testing to ascertain false awakenings.

Anything is possible in a lucid dream.

All lucid dreams are OBEs.

Entities You May Meet in the Fifth Dimension

1. **Departed Souls.** People who have died will be traveling through the fifth dimension and eventually move to the soul plane to select their future life.

2. **Near-death experiencers.** Those that clinically die but are revived spend their "death" time in the fifth dimension.

3. **Spirit guides.** These beings were once human and are more spiritually evolved than us. They assist us in our growth as a soul.

4. **Angels.** Messengers from the god-energy complex who were human and are perfect beings can be found here.

5. **Higher Self.** We all have a perfect component of our soul known as the Higher Self or superconscious mind. It assists us in our karmic cycle.

6. **Lower astral entities**. If you are unfortunate enough to end up in the lower astral plane, you may run into strange, evil beings who psychically attack us.

7. **Fellow fifth dimensional voyagers.** You may meet others like yourself who are practicing out-of-body techniques.

8. **Extraterrestrials.** There are some gatekeepers of the fifth dimension, such as pleiadians, who monitor portals to other dimensions. Grays and reptilian ETs can occupy regions of the lower astral plane too.

9. **Time travelers.** My research has shown that time travel on Earth will be discovered around the year 3050. Time travelers, or chrononauts, from the 31st century on do utilize the fifth dimension to move from one time era to the next.

Through the use of my Fifth Dimension self-hypnosis technique, you. can travel through hyperspace and explore parallel universes, go to the past or future and even communicate with a time traveler. Try this exercise from my Time Travelers Training Program CD album available from my website:

Fifth Dimension Time Travel

> **Now listen very carefully. I want you to imagine a bright white light coming down from above and entering the top of your head. Filling your entire body. See it, feel it and it becomes reality. Now imagine an aura of pure white light emanating from your heart region. Again surrounding your entire body. Protecting you. See it, feel it and it becomes reality. Now only your Masters and Guides and highly evolved loving entities who mean you well will be able to influence you during this or any other hypnotic session. You are totally protected by this aura of pure white light.**
> **In a few moments I am going to count from 1 to 20. As I do so you will feel yourself rising up to the superconscious mind level where**

you will be able to communicate with your Higher Self. Number 1, rising up. 2, 3, 4, rising higher. 5, 6, 7, letting information flow. 8, 9, 10, you are halfway there. 11, 12, 13, feel yourself rising even higher. 14, 15, 16, almost there. 17, 18, 19, number 20, you are there. Take a moment and orient yourself to the superconscious mind level.

Now I want you to merge with your Higher Self and be prepared to enter a wormhole. Take a few moments and perceive yourself actually entering and merging with the white light of your Higher Self. Do this now.

PLAY NEW AGE MUSIC FOR 2 MINUTES.*

Now that you have become one with your Higher Self, you are free to control this experience completely protected and out-of-your body. See a wormhole in front of you and enter it. This is a gateway into the Fifth Dimension. From here you can travel to the past, the future, or just remain in this Fifth Dimension hyperspace.

PLAY NEW AGE MUSIC FOR 4 MINUTES.

Very good. Now I want you to explore this wormhole we call the Fifth Dimension and travel anywhere in time and to any other dimension. Do this now.

---

*   Dr. Goldberg's website has New Age music CDs for all exercises.

PLAY NEW AGE MUSIC FOR 3 MINUTES.

Alright, you have done very well. In just a few moments I am going to count up from 1 to 5. When I reach the count of 5 you will be back in hyperspace from where you began this voyage. 1, you are returning to hyperspace, 2, moving closer, 3, halfway there, 4, almost there and 5, you are there. I'm going to count forwards from 1 to 5. When I reach the count of 5 you will be back in your physical body in the present. You will be able to remember everything you experienced and re-experienced. You'll feel very relaxed, refreshed, and be able to do whatever you have to planned for the rest of the day or evening. You'll feel very positive about what you've just experienced and very motivated about your confidence and ability to play this tape again to experience the Fifth Dimension. Alright now. 1, very, very deep, 2, you're getting a little bit lighter, 3, you're getting much, much lighter, 4, very, very light, 5 awaken. Wide awake and refreshed.

A Fifth Dimension Exercise to Lose Weight

Now listen very carefully. I want you to imagine a bright white light coming down from above and entering the top of your head, filling your entire body. See it, feel it and it becomes reality. Now imagine an aura of pure white light emanating from your heart region. Again, surrounding your entire body, protecting you. See it, feel it, and it becomes reality. Now only your Higher Self, Masters and Guides, and highly evolved loving entities who mean you well will be able to influence you during this or any other hypnotic session. You are totally protected by this aura of pure white light. In a few moments, I am going to count from 1 to 20. As I do so you will feel yourself rising up to the superconscious mind level where you will be able to receive information from your Higher Self. Number 1, rising up. 2,3, 4, rising higher. 5, 6, 7, letting information flow. 8, 9, 10, you are half-way there. 11,12, 13, feeling yourself rising even higher. 14, 15, 16 almost there. 17, 18 19 number 20, you are there. Take a moment and orient yourself to the superconscious mind level. Now I want you to merge with your Higher Self and be prepared to enter a black hole. Take a few moments and perceive yourself actually entering and merging with the white light of your Higher Self. Do this now.

PLAY NEW AGE MUSIC FOR 2 MINUTES.

You have now entered the fifth dimension in which your thought creates reality. Mentally see an image of yourself standing before you. This is your body exactly as you would like it to appear, exactly as you want that body to be, and as it has the possibility of being. Look at it more and more closely now, and it will be a realistic but ideal body image, one that you really could achieve, and one that you will achieve. And when you have a very clear image of your body as you would like to have it, keep observing that image, and make it a part of your own reality.

PLAY NEW AGE MUSIC FOR 4 MINUTES.

That ideal body image is becoming more and more real, you are seeing it very clearly, and seeing it in its full size and dimensions, and now you are going to step forward and into that body, you will find yourself in that body, so that you can try it out and make certain that it is just the body you do want to have, and if there is something you would like to change, then make those changes now.

Move around in that body, feel its strength and agility, its dynamic aliveness, its surging vitality, and make really certain that its appearance and all of its attributes are what you realistically desire. And, as you occupy that body, coming to know that body very well, your present physical body is going to be drawn into that new mold. You are moving already toward the realization of that ideal body image, and you will be doing whatever is needed to achieve that body you want to have.

PLAY NEW AGE MUSIC FOR 3 MINUTES.

All right, you have done very well. In just a few moments I am going to count up from 1 to 5. When I reach the count of 5 you will be back in hyperspace from where you began this voyage. 1, you are returning to hyperspace. 2, moving closer. 3, half-way there. 4, almost there, and 5, you are there. I'm going to count forward from 1 to 5. When I reach the count of 5 you will be back in your physical body in the present, you will be able to remember everything you experienced and re-experienced You'll feel very relaxed, refreshed, and able to do whatever you have planned for the rest of the day or evening. You'll feel very positive about what you've just experienced and very motivated about your confidence and ability to play this tape again to experience the Fifth Dimension. All right now. 1 very, very deep. 2, you're getting a little bit lighter. 3, you're getting much, much lighter. 4, very, very light. 5, awaken. Wide awake and refreshed.

CHAPTER 3

PARALLEL UNIVERSES

Before we discuss the fascinating world of parallel universes, consider the following statements by "experts" underestimating the value of technology:

- "Heavier-than-air flying machines are impossible." (Lord Kelvin, president, Royal Society, 1895).

- "The telephone has too many shortcomings to be seriously considered as a means of communication. The device is inherently of no value to us." (Western Union internal memo, 1876).
- "The wireless music box has no imaginable commercial value. Who would pay for a message sent to nobody in particular?" (David Sarnoff's associates, in response to his urgings for investment in radio in the 1920s).
- "Everything that can be invented has been invented." (Charles H. Duell, commissioner, U.S. Office of Patents, 1899).

Our Five Frequencies

The future consists of an unlimited number of parallel universes or frequencies, first demonstrated at Princeton University in 1957 by graduate student Hugh Everett III while completing his doctorate in quantum mechanics.

Although there theoretically are an unlimited number of these parallel universes, my experience since 1977 conducting over 6,000 progressions has shown that there are five main categories or paths.

Your five frequencies will be different than mine since we each have different levels of spiritual growth. One of these frequencies represents an ideal path, and in my hypnotherapy practice in Los Angeles I assist the patient to perceive all five paths and program them to their, ideal frequency. I refer to this as the "New You" technique.

There are duplicate yous and mes in each of these parallel universes. The exact outcome of these futures are different, depending on our actions and choices we make. Our consciousness can only recognize one frequency at a time. This is the reason you are not now aware of your other parallel selves in the present. We can describe these frequencies as follows:

Frequency	Summary
1	An average or slightly below average path and the one you are currently on
2	A very negative frequency. The worst path of the five
3	A slightly better than average path
4	The ideal path
5	A very good path, but not as fulfilling as number 4

I use this description to present a typical five-frequency paradigm. The numbers are arbitrary, and I chose 4 for the ideal path simply because it is my favorite number. Your ideal path may be number 2. In addition, some patients have reported two or more very negative paths. Individual variations do exist, but there is always an ideal frequency. Your ideal frequency in your current life is also your best path in a future incarnation.

PARALLEL UNIVERSES

When we think of the space our body occupies, we concern ourselves with the length, width and depth (height) of our physical structure. This constitutes our three-dimensional world. Time is added as the fourth dimension to this paradigm. In reality time is the fourth dimension of the space-time continuum.

The space-time continuum describes a simultaneity of all events in our life. To our concept of existence we must now add a fifth dimension of parallel lives occurring on parallel universes.

This fifth dimension is infinite, as quantum physics states that whenever we think of another possibility, we create another parallel universe. Although there are five broad categories or frequencies each parallel universe class has an infinite number of subdivisions.

To comprehend this concept, consider all five of our parallel selves in the same "location" at the same "time." This is a type of hologram. Each parallel universe is simply a characteristic, or optional path, of our five-dimensional being. When we think of a past or future event in our current parallel universe as a frequency (the one that we are aware of at this moment)it is a part of history (existing in simultaneous time) and a component of probable parallel universes (never ending, as we continually create additional universes).

This supernatural or beyond physicality of a five-dimensional paradigm cannot appear to us within our three-dimensional world unless we enter into an altered state of consciousness (as in hypnosis, OBEs or meditation) and globally assess these dimensions.

Another example of this simultaneity of time is that each parallel universe is part of an expanding universe (an expansion that is not occurring in physical space), so it doesn't take up time per se. Every event takes place at the same moment in time. There is no beginning or end to these occurrences, as we have been misprogrammed to believe.

We can think of physical space as a representation of mental or inner space of consciousness. This mental space contains an infinite number of probable events. Some of these possibilities are contrary to our beliefs and are less likely to occur in our present awareness parallel universe.

It is our consciousness that creates our reality in the form of these five major paths or parallel universes. Each of these worlds exist at the same time and location. When we choose to observe them (such as in hypnosis), and only when we observe them, do they become part of our reality.

Each and every one of these parallel universes contains yous and mes (parallel lives) superimposed upon each other. This applies to past lives, our current lifetime and future incarnations. Can we alter the past? Quantum physics says we can, depending on the degree of observability. The more observed an event is, the less we can change it.

Each universe has the same environment and people, but the actions produce different results. I use the term paragression to describe exploring parallel lives in the fifth dimension through hypnosis.

A Parallel Life Case

In 1997 when 16-year-old Tonya asked me to train her to leave her body, I didn't realize just how successful she would be. One Sunday afternoon Tonya used my Custom Design Your Own Destiny album and traveled to a parallel universe. She first arrived back in time to the year 1968 and noted that Robert F. Kennedy not only was not assassinated, but was elected President. The U.S. pulled out of Vietnam by 1970. There was no Nixon presidency or Watergate, the Soviet Union collapsed in 1986, and the economic picture of the world was bright in most every country.

When Tonya arrived back in 1997, she looked the same but felt somewhat odd. Still in this parallel universe, she simply could not relate to her mother, who looked the same but was yet "different."

Upon reentering our current universe following the termination of her OBE and hypnotic trance, Tonya went to speak to her mother. Her mother asked her what was wrong with her all afternoon. She said Tonya acted so different that she almost didn't recognize her own daughter. What really happened was that Tonya changed places with her parallel life on another universe for 3 hours. Each of her parallel lives felt out of place as did her mothers in both universes. Tonya was literally beside herself.

Rosie worked as an executive secretary for an east coast public relations firm. She was underpaid and her boss who owned this small firm, regularly abused her. She did all of his "dirty work" and was never acknowledged for her efforts.

This mousy-looking, shy, and very insecure woman wanted a new life. She was also having an affair with her boss and was afraid to end it. Her position did pay her more than she could earn elsewhere, and she desperately needed the money.

There was plenty of room here for empowerment. Rosie was trained with superconscious mind taps, then guided into her five future frequencies. The one she selected showed her moving to Florida and eventually buying into a radio station in that sunshine state.

I last saw Rosie in 1984. Four years later, she called my office and wanted to stop by to see me. She didn't have a problem but just wanted to say hello. I agreed to this meeting and could not believe my eyes when she came in.

This mousy woman had metamorphosed into an assertive, beautiful, and empowered soul. She had lost weight, changed her hairstyle and color, and now beamed with confidence. In fact, she came into town to visit her family. Rosie now resided in Florida and was part owner of a radio station there. She was a successful and fulfilled soul, well on her way to a very bright future. You might say her life turned out to be a "rosy scenario."

Andrea wanted to view the future of her current life in order to resolve issues concerning her relationship with her husband, psychosomatic illnesses, and their financial future. She suffered from rheumatoid arthritis, back pain, and insomnia. In addition, she was rapidly drifting apart from her husband (Roger).

Andrea was initially oriented and trained with superconscious mind taps prior to the age progression. During one of her progression frequencies, she was shot and killed in her hometown of Detroit. The frequency Andrea chose showed that she was to overcome her psychosomatic illnesses, while Roger would sell his business to become a highly paid consultant. Their relationship markedly improved on this path and they lived in Florida.

These age progressions were conducted in 1990, and according to my March, 1995 conversation with her, these events transpired. Prior to my call, Andrea wrote me a rather nice letter notifying me of her move to Florida and updating me as to her progress.

One final side note here concerns the shooting that Andrea fortunately avoided. It seems that on the day she would have been shot (had she stayed on the frequency she was on when she came to my office), someone was shot and killed in Detroit, and at the location she described.

If you would like to try my New You technique to view your parallel universes and switch to your ideal one, order my Custom Design Your Own Destiny CD album from my website.

My research has revealed the following events occurring in parallel universes:

- The British win the American Revolutionary War and kill George Washington.

- Hitler wins World War II and develops the atomic bomb.

- Joshua is defeated in the Battle of Jericho and there is no Israel. No monotheistic religions (Judaism, Christianity and Islam) are established.

- A comet hits the earth in 1999 as predicted by Nostradamus and many millions of people die.

Try this script to explore one of your parallel lives:

Now listen very carefully. I want you to imagine a bright white light coming down from above and entering the top of your head, filling your entire body. See it, feel it and it becomes reality. Now imagine an aura of pure white light emanating from your heart region.   Again, surrounding your entire body, protecting you. See it, feel it, and it becomes reality. Now only your Higher Self, Masters and Guides, and highly evolved loving entities who mean you well will be able to influence you during this or any other hypnotic session. You are totally protected by this aura of pure white light. In a few moments, I am going to count from 1 to 20. As I do so you will feel yourself rising up to the superconscious mind level where you will be able to receive information from your Higher Self. Number 1, rising up. 2, 3, 4, rising higher. 5, 6, 7, letting information flow. 8.9,10, you are half-way there. 11,12, 13, feeling yourself rising even higher. 14, 15, 16, almost there. 17, 18, 19, number 20, you are there. Take a moment and orient yourself to the superconscious mind level. Now I want you to merge with your Higher Self and be prepared to enter a black hole. Take a few moments and perceive yourself actually cntering and merging with the white light of your Higher Self. Do this now.

PLAY NEW AGE MUSIC FOR 2 MINUTES.

Now that you have become one with your Higher Self, you are free to control this experience, completely protected and out of your body. See a black hole in front of you and enter it. This is a gateway into the Fifth Dimension. From here you can travel to parallel universes and the future. Focus on meeting other Souls in this hyper-universe. Take a few moments and open yourself to encountering other entities. You are perfectly safe and protected, and you will only attract positive people and souls into your awareness. Do this now.

PLAY NEW AGE MUSIC FOR 3 MINUTES.

Very good. At this time I want you to explore one of your parallel lives in another frequency. You will look the same, but the events on this path will be different from the path you are currently on. Carry this fifth dimension exercise all the way to the end of your life. You are perfectly safe. Do this now.

PLAY NEW AGE MUSIC FOR 4 MINUTES.

All right, you have done very well. In just a few moments I am going to count up from 1 to 5. When I reach the count of 5 you will be back in hyperspace from where you began this voyage. 1, you are returning to hyperspace. 2, moving closer. 3, half-way there. 4, almost there, and 5, you are there. I'm going to count forward from 1 to 5. When I reach the count of 5 you will be back in your physical body in the present, you will be able to remember everything you experienced and re-experienced. You'll feel very relaxed, refreshed, and able to do whatever you have planned for the rest of the day or evening. You'll feel very positive about what you've just experienced and very motivated about your

confidence and ability to play this tape again to experience the Fifth Dimension and parallel universes. All right now. 1 very, very deep. 2, you're getting a little bit lighter. 3, you're getting much, much lighter. 4, very, very light. 5, awaken. Wide awake and refreshed.

A Parallel Self Case

Not only do we have past and future lives, but our soul (which is energy in the form of electromagnetic radiation) is capable of occupying more than one physical body in our current frequency. We refer to this as a parallel self.

When we perceive these parallel universes in progression therapy, the purpose is to choose the ideal one for your spiritual growth. These universes are in the future of our current life or in future lifetimes in centuries to come. In rare instances, an individual can meet with another body in their current life whose energy (soul) is identical with theirs. Both of these souls originated from a common "ancestor." We call this common ancestor the "Oversoul." This is not the same as frequency 2, 3, 4, or 5. You are living your life in a body now and part of your soul is living in another body on this very same frequency.

A male patient of mine (Charles) described his soul living now in another body of a man named "Winchester." This was apparently a nickname, and Winchester was a rather large lumberjack-type fellow with red hair and with a predisposition to wearing plaid clothes. Charles never mentioned Winchester to anyone but me.

Charles had blonde hair and was a thin five eight inch academic-looking gentleman. Six months after this parallel life was brought out, Charles' cousin (Janine) across the country had an emergency and her car was stuck in a ditch on a deserted road. Shortly after this occurred, a pickup truck came by and the driver towed Janine's car back on the road.

CHAPTER 3

This kind gentleman was a rather large man with red hair and wore a plaid shirt and a plaid jacket. He introduced himself as Winchester. Janine felt she knew this man, but he denied ever meeting her. She didn't realize it at the time but Janine met Charles' parallel self in her current universe.

We all have parallel selves but most of us will never meet them. The following figures explain how this occurs:

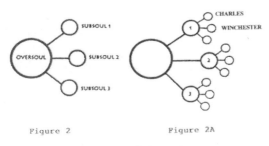

Figure 2   Figure 2A

The Oversoul Concept

In Figure 2, we see that an oversoul splits into three subsouls. Each subsoul further divides itself into three additional subsubsouls and so on. If our Charles' and Janine's soul originated from Subsoul 1 (as in Figure 2A) you can note the common background for the respective energy component (soul).

This concept (known as the Oversoul Concept) helps explain the world's population and the lack of virgin (new) souls today. One oversoul dividing into just three subsouls and each subsoul also occupying three physical bodies would result in the same original oversoul occupying over 1.5 million bodies in just 13 generations (390 years).

Try this exercise to experience one of your parallel selves:

Now listen very carefully. I want you to imagine a bright white light coming down from above and entering the top of your head. Filling your entire body. See it, feel it and it becomes

reality. Now imagine an aura of pure white light emanating from your heart region. Again surrounding your entire body. Protecting you. See it, feel it and it becomes reality. Now only your masters and guides and highly evolved loving entities who mean you well will be able to influence you during this or any other hypnotic session. You are totally protected by this aura of pure white light. Focus carefully on my voice as your subconscious mind's memory banks has memories of all past, present and future and parallel lifetimes. This tape will help guide you into a life in a different body than you currently occupy, but in this same time period. We call this a parallel self.

Some of your parallel selves may have died or crossed onto spirit. You may be a mere infant, a different race or sex. Allow your Higher Self to assist you by choosing a parallel self that will result in the greatest amount of spiritual growth and understanding.

Your superconscious mind or Higher Self will now assist you in selecting this parallel self to explore. Shortly I am going to be counting forward from one to twenty. As I-count forward from one to twenty you are going to imagine yourself moving through a tunnel. You're going to go through the tunnel and this will take you into a parallel self. On the count of 20 you will perceive yourself in this parallel self. Your subconscious and superconscious mind levels have all the knowledge and information that you desire. Carefully and comfortably feel yourself moving into this parallel self with each count from one to twenty. Listen carefully now. Number one, feel yourself now moving into this very, very deep and dark tunnel. Two, three, farther and farther into the tunnel. Four, five, six, the tunnel is very, very dark. It is a little bit disorienting but you know you're moving into this parallel self. Seven, eight, nine, it's more stable now and you feel comfortable, you feel almost as if you're floating, as you're rising up and into this parallel self. Ten, eleven, twelve, the tunnel is now getting a little bit lighter and you can perceive a light at the end, another white light just like the white light that is surrounding you.

Thirteen, fourteen, fifteen. Now you are almost there. Focus carefully. You can perceive a door in front of you. The door will be opened in just a few moments and you will see yourself as a parallel self.

The words sleep now and rest will always detach yourself from any scene you are experiencing and allow you to wait further instructions. Sixteen, seventeen. It's very
bright now and you are putting your hands on the door.

Eighteen, you open the door, nineteen, you step into this parallel self. Number twenty. Carefully focus on your surroundings, look around you, see what you perceive. Can you perceive yourself? Can you perceive other people around you? Focus on the environment. What does it look like? Carefully focus on this. Use your complete objectivity. Block out any information from the past that might have interfered with the quality of the scene. Use only what your subconscious and superconscious mind level will observe. Now take a few moments, focus carefully on the scene, find out where you are, what are you doing, why are you there. Take a few moments, let the scene manifest itself.

PLAY NEW AGE MUSIC FOR 3 MINUTES.*

Now focus very carefully on what year this is. Think for a moment. Numbers will appear before your inner eyes. You will have knowledge of the year that you are in right now. Carefully focus on this year and these numbers. They will appear before you. Use this as an example of other information that you are going to obtain. I want you to perceive this scene completely, carry it through to completion. I want you to perceive exactly where you are, who you are, the name, the date, the place. I want you to carry these scenes to completion, follow them through carefully for the next few moments. The scene will become clear and you will perceive the sequence of what exactly is happening to you.

PLAY NEW AGE MUSIC FOR 3 MINUTES.

You've done very well. Now you are going to move to another event. I want you to focus on a different experience in this same parallel self. Perceive what is going on and why this is important to you. Perceive the year, the environment, the presence of others. Let the information flow.

---

* Dr. Goldberg's website has New Age music for these exercises.

PLAY NEW AGE MUSIC FOR 3 MINUTES.

As you perceive the details of the next scene, focus also, in on your purpose. Your purpose in this parallel self and how it is affecting your karmic subcycle. Focus in on what you are learning, what you are unable to learn. Perceive any sequence of events that led up to this situation. Let the information flow surrounding this all important parallel self event now.

PLAY NEW AGE MUSIC FOR 3 MINUTES.

Sleep now and rest. You've done very well. Now I want you to rise to the superconscious mind level to evaluate this parallel self experience and apply this knowledge to your current life and situations. One, rising up, 2 rising higher, 3 half way there, 4 almost there, number 5 - you are there. Let your Masters and Guides assist you in making the most out of this experience. Do this now.

PLAY NEW AGE MUSIC FOR 3 MINUTES.

Alright now. Sleep now and rest. You did very, very well. Listen very carefully. I'm going to count backwards now from 5 - 1. This time when I reach 1 you will be back in your present life, you will be able to remember everything you experienced and re-experienced you'll feel very relaxed refreshed, you'll be able to do whatever you have to planned for the rest of the day or evening. You'll feel very positive about what you've just experienced and very motivated about your confidence and ability to play this tape again to experience additional parallel self events. Alright now. I'm going to count forwards from 1 to 5 and when I reach the count of 5 you will be wide awake, relaxed and refreshed. Number 1 very, very deep. Number 2 you are getting a little bit lighter. Number 3 half way there. Number 4, very, very light. Number 5 awaken.

CHAPTER 4

TELEPORTATION

"Beam me up Scottie" requires no explanation for those who have followed the original Star Trek television series and the early feature films of the exploits of the crew of the Enterprise. What the engineer Scott was initiating was a form of teleportation in which a human body was dematerialized from one location and rematerialized at another.

Scottie used a transporter apparatus to bring about his form of fictionalized teleportation. Recently Austrian physicists successfully teleported subatomic light parties (photons) at a distance of a few feet. This paradigm was considered impossible by Einstein. We can experience teleportation through hypnosis without any machine whatsoever.

Teleportation is the process of physically relocating a body from one place to another site without touching it in any way, or using any mechanical device. What we find in a true teleportation is that the physical body disappears from one location and subsequently reappears in a different spot in an instant, often accompanied by a "pop" sound. It does not dematerialize into sparkles of light.

Teleportation is often confused with out-of-body experiences (OBEs) . An OBE is the movement of the soul or subconscious (electromagnetic radiation) from one location or dimension to another, while the entire physical body is relocated in teleportation. Theoretical physics supports the contention that tears in the space-time continuum would allow for us to travel backward, forward, and sideways in time. It must be remembered that in each case the fifth dimension is entered, and the principles of hyperspace apply.

We can experience teleportation during the dream state. It differs from regular dreams and lucid dreams in that your body physically leaves the bed and travels to another location on a different dimension.

If you are observing someone actually being teleported, you would see their body slowly fade away and disappear. Nothing else in the environment would be altered. The person undergoing teleportation would experience an increase in their energy vibrating at high speed, accompanied by a tingling, buzzing sensation and/or a feeling of spiraling upward. Often a "pop" sound emanates from the top of the head, as I previously mentioned.

Teleportation can take place in three different ways. The first is a spontaneous teleportation. You may have had the experience of performing some chore that you had done thousands of times before and sensing for a moment that you were someplace else. Another possibility is walking down a street, or jogging, and realizing that you are much farther from your origin than was possible over the period of time in question.

The second type of teleportation is one that is directed during your sleep state. This experience differs from regular or lucid dreams in that you are not confronted with symbols or merely your subconscious transported to dream world. Your physical body in teleportation has physically relocated to the astral plane, or other dimension. This memory of a true teleportation is clear and accompanied by recall of physical sensations. Most dreams are hazy and leave us confused as to their meaning.

A consciously directed teleportation comprises the third group. In the beginning you will find that you wind up in places far from your goal. This low level of accuracy improves dramatically with regular practice. When you return to your place of origin, you will again hear that "pop" sound. Your body travels at the speed of light, so distance is of no significance.

In order to successfully experience teleportation, you need to focus your mind and block out all other distractions. It is only your limiting beliefs that will prevent you from experiencing this unique form of travel.

Your body must be well rested to assure success. You will find it easiest to teleport at night. Since your body has had many spontaneous teleportation experiences while dreaming, the night is a natural environment and time for the novice teleporter.

I also recommend you teleport to secluded places to avoid shocking other people when you materialize in front of them. Always act as if you are already in your desired location when practicing teleportation. See yourself as if you were viewing this new place form inside your body (first person perspective), not as if it were a dream or a movie. Make sure you see, feel and sense yourself in this new spot.

The natural tendency is to hold your breath during a teleportation. You must resist that temptation and breathe consciously by taking slow, deep breaths. Since teleportation is a mental activity, we must not deprive our brain cells of its needed oxygen. You will feel lightheaded, with a swirling and upward spiraling sensation during this process. Occasionally, people report nausea during their initial stages of relocating. This will disappear quickly and be prevented by proper breathing.

Others report a sexual sensation in their body. Sometimes a feeling of tightness across the eyebrows (third eye area) is described. Your perception at your desired location will appear as if you were looking at your location through a keyhole. This disappears with practice. Always state clearly your intention to travel to a certain location or visit a certain individual. You do not want to imply that this is a desire that can fail, but a declaration of an empowered soul who is confident about succeeding in this venture.

For example, state "I intend to teleport to Tahiti." Also state "I intend to visit Janine in Paris this afternoon." You must always trust yourself and your Higher Self and acknowledge your ability to teleport anywhere in the universe or to any other dimension.

There is a famous story of a man from Kansas who in 1879 took a walk following his dinner at a local restaurant and was never seen again. He had gone to the general store earlier that day and had a receipt establishing his name, his location and the date.

In 1950, a man oddly dressed was run over and killed in Times Square in New York City by a cab driver. This man was identified as the very same man from 1879 Kansas and this story was reported in *Collier's Magazine* in the early 1950s. Teleportation is the only explanation for this event. It was a New York city cab driver, not teleportation, that killed the gentleman from Kansas. We shall see that teleportation may involve time travel in addition to a change in location.

Levitation

Levitation is a localized form of teleportation in which the individual rises off the ground and hovers a few inches to several feet above the ground. We see biblical examples in the walking across the Sea of Galilee by Jesus and Peter. Other Catholic religious figures that were known to levitate were St. Teresa of Avila, St. Francis of Assisi, and St. Joseph of Cupertino. A complete teleportation may be produced from a levitating body.

St. Joseph's case was particularly well documented. His levitations were witnessed by Pope Urban VIII. The "flying friar" was the nickname for St. Joseph, due to his frequent teleporting. One report described him assisting several construction workers who were unable to lift and properly place a heavy iron cross on a local church. The flying friar "rose like a bird into the air" and with no trouble lifted the cross and set it into its appropriate location.

He would suddenly cry out and fly up in the air, and so disrupted church services that he was barred from public worship.

St. Ignatius Loyola was known to hover just above the ground while meditating. St. Adolphus Liguori was raised into the air in front of a whole congregation in 1777. Some levitators, like Passitea Crogi, a Sienese nun who died in 1615, were seen traveling a considerable distance just above the ground.

A Spanish nun known as Mary of Agreda never physically left her convent to travel to the New World, but during the 17th century teleported over 500 times to New Mexico to convert the Jumano Indians between 1620-1631.

In 1622, Father Alonzo de Benavides, of the Isolita Mission in New Mexico, had written to Pope Urban VIII and to Philip IV of Spain asking who had pre-empted him in his mission to convert the Jumano Indians. The Jumanos themselves declared their knowledge of Christianity to have come from a "lady in blue," a European nun who had left them crosses, rosaries and a chalice which they used for celebrating Mass. This chalice was believed to have come from Mary's convent at Agreda. Mary's visits to New Mexico were documented by the logs of Spanish conquistadors, accounts of several Spanish tribes a thousand miles apart, records of French explorers and several historians of the Southwest of the United States. Since she never physically left Spain, the only explanation is teleportation. As a youth, Mary was almost condemned as a witch for her frequent levitations.

Most levitations seem to occur while the levitator is in a trance or ecstasy. The phenomenon is not exclusive to Catholic saints.

Daniel Home was a medium who lived during the nineteenth century and levitated in front of Emperor Napoleon III and Mark Twain. Home began his teleporting at the age of nineteen, with a series of spontaneous levitations at home witnessed by his family.

Levitation is described in the Indian Vedas as a *laghima*, an unknown power that is part of the physiological makeup and acts as a centrifugal force strong enough to counteract all gravitational pull. Charles Fort noted that when he reported objects falling from the sky, they appeared to descend slowly, as if under the influence of some anti-gravitational force. Fort drew attention to the curious lack of injury to most falling creatures, as if they too had had the benefit of a slow descent, or levitation.

A Time Traveler Meets Her Younger Self

In 1996, a 72-year-old woman came to my Los Angeles office for past life regression hypnotherapy and reported a most unusual incident that took place a few months earlier. This patient, whom I shall refer to as Eva, always wears a yellow scarf and has since her teenage years.

Eva is a slender woman now, but had a weight problem until she was about 50. A few months ago, she went to a local mall in her home town to do some clothes shopping and wore her customary yellow scarf. Eva has always lived in the same city. She went to her favorite department store and saw a woman who looked exactly as she would have 30 years ago!

This young woman in her 40s was overweight and wore a dark brown miniskirt, along with a yellow scarf and light green blouse. There was a blue ink stain on the back of this skirt. Eva recalled that she had such a skirt and it was her favorite. The only problem with it was that it had a blue ink stain on the back of it!

Eva approached this woman and stood right in front of her. She got a good look at her and clearly identified this person as herself as she looked 30 years ago. As she was about to speak to this individual, the younger Eva appeared to fade away and disappear. This was witnessed by another woman who immediately ran out of the store.

Eva hadn't thought of that brown miniskirt in many years. She doesn't have any pictures of herself at that age, but her family does. After researching family photo albums, Eva finally found a picture of herself in her early 40s wearing a yellow scarf, the brown miniskirt and the exact same light green blouse she saw on her younger self in the mall.

My explanation of this event is that Eva somehow teleported herself at age 42 from 1966 to 1996. I suspect they could have talked to each other, but the universe had other plans. The young Eva teleported back to 1966 in the same way she arrived. I asked Eva if she ever recalled such an incident 30 years ago. She stated that one afternoon she did "blackout" for an hour or so, but all medical tests were negative. There never was another similar occurrence.

For an hour in 1966, Eva became a time traveler who traveled ahead 30 years and returned to her point of origin. Perhaps she entered a tear in the fabric of space-time.

A Teleporting Time Traveler Saves Two Lives

Two nine year old classmates were walking home from school in Texas when suddenly an older teenager around 18 ran up to them and pushed both of them aside. This teenager was wearing a light blue tennis outfit and just as she pushed both of these girls (Brenda and Amy) aside, a car driven by a drunken teenager jumped the curb and would have killed these girls by hitting them head on. As Brenda and Amy turned to thank this teenage girl, the older girl disappeared!

Ten years later I worked with Amy who related this story. What brought this to her attention was that she remained friends with Brenda and they recently decided to play tennis. Amy picked up Brenda at her parent's home and saw Brenda in the exact same blue tennis outfit worn by the teenager who saved both of their lives ten years earlier. Brenda told Amy that she blacked out for a short time earlier that day and had a dream that she saved the lives of two younger girls.

Amy now realized that it was the 19 year old Brenda that saved them. Brenda had entered into a tear in the fabric of space-time and traveled back in time 10 years to save herself and Amy from the drunken teenager in the car.

Brenda had become a time traveler deep in the heart of Texas by way of teleportation.

CHAPTER 4

The Teleportation of Two Brothers

Alfredo and Paolo Pansini of Ruvo, Italy had a long history of teleporting during the early 1900s. When Alfredo was seven he frequently vanished suddenly from his house and reappeared in various areas of town or nearby towns, often in a dazed state. Paolo would also teleport to other locales.

This case was documented by Joseph Lappeni, a medical advisor to Popes Leo XIII and Pius X. To test these boys, a Bishop Bernardi Pasquale locked them in the bedroom and sealed all doors and windows. Even with these precautions both boys disappeared within a few minutes.

Vivian's Teleportation

I worked with Vivian with OBE and teleportation training techniques. One afternoon she was in her car with her physically abusive boyfriend. They got into an argument and her boyfriend threw open the passenger door and pushed Vivian out into incoming traffic. Vivian twisted her ankle and could not run.

All she could think of, as a car speeding in her direction, was the post-hypnotic suggestion I gave her to enter into hypnosis and teleport. She concentrated on her living room and the next thing that happened was a car slammed on its brakes right in front of her.

She was observed by both the driver of that car and her boyfriend to disappear. The car passed right through the spot Vivian was standing in and should have hit her. The next thing Vivian became aware of was sitting on her living room couch with a sore ankle.

Vivian teleported from the busy street to her apartment. There is no other logical explanation to explain this event. Later we worked on finding a soul mate for her and, six months following her breakup with her boyfriend, she met Mr. Right. They were married a year later and today are quite happy.

TELEPORTATION

Cases Involving Clouds, Gases, Fogs, and Mists

We have many reported cases of people being teleported from place to place in the presence of clouds, mists, fogs, and gases that seem to appear suddenly from nowhere, condense around a vehicle or person, and result in the sudden vanishing of the objects or people it encircles.

Argentinian Cases

Argentina appears to be the site of several fifth-dimensional openings or tears in the fabric of space-time. A businessman was driving south from Buenos Aires to Bahía Blanca in 1959 when suddenly a white cloud appeared out of nowhere and transported this man to a road unfamiliar to him.

As his car was not teleported with him, the businessman asked a truck. driver where he was. It turns out that he was now in Salta, over 800 miles from Bahía Blanca. After contacting the local authorities, it was discovered that this man's car was exactly where he last recalled it to be, and the engine was still running.

Another case took place in 1968. In May of that year two cars containing family members on their way from a family gathering at Chascomus left Chascomus and were headed south toward Maipu. Traveling in one car were Dr. Gerardo Vidal and his wife Raffo of Buenos Aires.

The other couple reached Maipu with no problem, but the Vidal car never arrived. The Vidals called the other couple in Maipu two days later stating that they were unharmed but confused. A dense fog had appeared out of nowhere and engulfed their car. Their destination was an isolated country road in an unknown location.

The Vidals shortly discovered that they were in Mexico, over 4,000 miles away! To substantiate this fog, a man was admitted to a hospital in Maipu on the same night the Vidals were teleported; this man confirmed the presence of the fog. His experience with the fog was for just a few moments, but when it left, the watches of all those in the car had suddenly stopped. Teleportation is the most logical explanation of the Vidals relocation to Mexico.

British Cases of Teleportation

In October 1974, John Avis, his wife Sue, and their three children were returning home from a trip through a deserted countryside near London. A green fog encircled their car and sparks flew out of their car radio.

John pulled out the car radio wires and everyone soon felt a bump and a jolt as the car seemed to leave the ground and fall back to Earth suddenly. The mist was now gone and they soon arrived home, but two hours later than they were supposed to!

On February 9, 1988 a truck driver was walking along a road near Oswestry in Shropshire at 8:00 A.M. on a clear, sunny morning. He noticed an elderly woman with a dog walking alongside her.

Suddenly a yellow-white cloud emitting a noise like a motor appeared. The dog ran into this cloud and vanished. This rotating cloud, thirty feet in diameter, soon began to dissipate and vanished altogether. The dog lay on the ground panting heavily, soaking wet, and with bloodshot eyes. It recovered but died soon afterward of "natural causes."

The Bermuda Triangle

Two small areas that have been the scenes of more disappearances than all the rest of the world put together are known as the "Bermuda Triangle" and the "Devil's Sea." One lies in the Atlantic off the east coast of the United States, the other in the Pacific, southeast of Japan. We will discuss the former.

The term "Bermuda Triangle" was coined by Vincent Gaddis, who also called it the "Triangle of Death." Gaddis was among the first to notice the incredible number of ships and aircraft disappearing in this relatively small area. Well over a hundred such disappearances have been recorded, with the loss of more than a thousand lives. Most of these mysteries have occurred since 1945, and the disappearances have been total. Not a single body nor a fragment of wreckage from the vanished crafts has ever been recovered. The infamous Sargasso Sea lies within the Bermuda Triangle.

In 1609 a ship called the *Sea Venture* was shipwrecked off the coast of Bermuda, on its way to Virginia bringing settlers to the New World. One of the longboats of the *Sea Venture* set out to the mainland of America to enlist aid. It was never seen again.

Five Spanish treasure ships encountered storms in this region and disappeared in 1750, and a search of the area turned up no evidence or any wreckage.

The number of lost ships and planes from this area east of Florida engendered even more interest from the U.S. government when Flight 19 vanished on December 5, 1945. Five Avenger torpedo bombers left Fort Lauderdale Naval Air Station on a training exercise that should have taken them over the Grand Bahama Island, then southwest back to their base.

Lieutenant Charles G. Carroll Taylor led this flight. He was an experienced aviator, but less than two hours after takeoff (2:10 P.M.) he sent the following radio message to the base: "Both my compasses are out....I'm over land, but it's broken. I'm sure I'm in the Keys, but I don't know how far down and I don't know how to get to Fort Lauderdale." This message was interrupted by Lieutenant Robert Cox, who was flying over Fort Lauderdale on another exercise.

A transmission followed: "'All planes close up tight...we will have to ditch unless landfall...when the first man gets down to ten gallons we will all land in the water together." A five-day search covering 250,000 square miles of ocean revealed no trace of Flight 19.

A 400-page naval inquiry record could not answer several questions. Why did both of Taylor's compasses fail shortly after they were checked out in the preflight inspection? Even though the northernmost Bahamas look much like the Florida Keys from the air, how did the airmen become convinced that the first leg of their flight had taken them so far south rather than east? The Navy could never explain how a planned two-hour training flight became a wandering, five-hour journey to nowhere. They conducted over 930 sorties over the area and found no evidence of a crash.

British airliners, the *Star Ariel* and the *Star Tiger*, vanished in January 1949 while flying over the Sargasso Sea. All searches again turned up no physical evidence of these two planes. One interesting observation in reference to the disappearance of the Star Ariel was that both a British commercial plane and an American bomber reported sighting a strange light and a floating object that reflected the moonlight in the sea about 300 miles south of Bermuda. It was in the same area that *Star Ariel* had disappeared.

There is at least one incident on file of a pilot who survived the unexplained forces of the Bermuda triangle. Chuck Wakely, a chart plane pilot, in 1962 was returning from a solo flight from Nassau to Miami. He climbed to 8,000 feet, leveled off, and settled back for a routine run. Soon he noticed a faint glow on the wings of his plane.

As this glow increased in intensity it became impossible to read his instruments, so he used manual control of the plane. The wings glowed bluish green and looked fuzzy. Wakely had to release his controls, but was saved from disaster as the glow began to fade. When the glow finally died out the instruments began to work properly again and Wakely was able to make a safe landing at his destination. One possible explanation for these cases is teleporting into the fifth dimension.

The Teleportation of a Spanish Soldier

On October 25,1593, a Spanish soldier suddenly appeared on the plaza in front of the palace in Mexico City. His uniform was unlike that of the other palace guards, and he carried a different type of gun.

When questioned later, this bewildered soldier stated that his orders were to guard the governor's palace in Manila! He insisted that he was from Manila, which is over 9,000 miles away and required at least several weeks travel time in the sixteenth century.

To prove his claim, he stated that the governor of Manila, Don Gomez Perez das Marinas, had been murdered the previous night. Mexico City authorities placed the soldier in prison. He was also visited by a local priest who performed an exorcism to remove alleged demons.

Two months later a ship arrived from the Philippines with news that the governor had indeed been murdered on the precise date claimed by this soldier! He was then released and sent back to his unit in Manila. This case is interesting in that it was documented by the local authorities and the Catholic Church!

Linda was trained in the art of teleportation when she came to my Los Angeles office in 1992. She lived in a very small town in the southeastern part of the United States. There was only one hair dresser in her town and Monday was her day off.

One rather humid Monday summer afternoon Linda teleported herself to Chicago and had her hair done. Her husband drove the only car this family had to work, as they lived in an isolated farm community. He questioned her on how she was able to get her hair done on a Monday.

Since he saw her that morning in her old hair style, Linda was uncomfortable. She knew her husband would question her sanity if she disclosed her teleportation incident. She simply said it was her little secret. and someday this story would be related to him. He scratched his head and never brought this topic up again.

The Teleportation of Charles W. Ingersoll

In 1948 businessman Charles W. Ingersoll of Cloquet, Minnesota decided to go to the Grand Canyon on a vacation. He was unable to make this trip that year due to his business responsibilities. Finally, in 1955 Ingersoll purchased a brand new Bosley 35mm slide camera and went to the Grand Canyon in Arizona.

65

Shortly after his return Charles went to his local photography store and purchased a travelogue film of the Grand Canyon. To his amazement he observed himself leaning over the rim of the Grand Canyon *taking pictures with his 1955 Bosley camera!*

This film was produced by Castle Films and copyrighted in 1948. There were 1948 automobiles (none more recent) and people were dressed in clothing styles characteristic of that year. There is no possibility of footage being added to the film, as the quality was all the same and the store owner testified to the fact the film he sold Ingersoll had been on the shelf for years untouched.

The only logical explanation is that Charles W. Ingersoll entered into the fifth dimension by way of a tear in the fabric of space-time and teleported back in time from 1955 to 1948 (with his 1955 camera) in time to be filmed at the Grand Canyon as part of Castle Film's travelogue.

Time Slips

A time slip is an event where it appears that some other era has briefly intruded on the present. A time slip seems to be spontaneous in nature and localization, but there are places on the planet that seem to be more prone than others to time slip events. Also, some people may be more inclined to experience time slips than others.

There are many reported cases of people who have teleported back in time to observe real events. I feel these are natural phenomenon, that under the right conditions and location, can briefly produce a doorway to another time and place. Here is one of the most documented examples of this principle.

In August, 1901 two English teachers went on holiday to Paris. These were Anne Moberly, principal of St. Hugh's college in Oxford, and Dr. Eleanor Jourdain. They visited Versailles and began looking for the Petit Trianon (a small chateau in Versailles given to Marie Antoinette by Louis XVI in 1774). As they wandered around the grounds, they both felt strange and observed two men dressed in long grayish-green coats with small three-cornered hats. These men directed the ladies to the Petit Trianon.

As they approached a small country house with shuttered windows and terraces on either side, a woman was sitting on the lawn with her back to the house. This woman wore a summer dress and a large white hat and was drawing on a large sheet of paper. The English teachers recognized this woman as Marie Antoinette!

Another fact these women noticed was the music they heard during this experience. They wrote it down, along with sketches of the Petit Trianon. Nobody at the time believed their story when they returned home. Experts said that no such music was ever played at that time.

Research revealed that on October 5, 1789 Marie Antoinette had been at the Petit Trianon when she first learned that a mob from Paris was marching toward the palace. Recently in Paris, music manuscripts were found that had been composed for Marie Antoinette's 34th birthday in 1789 and played on that day. This music was identical to what the school teachers reported.

Another journal was uncovered written by one of the ladies of Marie Antoinette's court. One entry read, "Two women dressed in strange clothes wandered unexpectedly onto the grounds." The features of the landscape depicted by the two English ladies matched those which actually existed in 1789, but not in 1901.

It is of interest that there were electrical storms all over Europe in August of 1901. Perhaps this storm opened up a portal and allowed these two women to teleport back in time from 1901 to 1789 and back again. In more recent times others have had similar, but less impressive experiences in Versailles.

The late paranormal and celebrity biologist Ivan T. Sanderson, his wife and an assistant were driving in a remote area of Haiti when their car became bogged down in a pool of mud. They abandoned the vehicle and began to walk until exhausted. Sanderson described the scene as follows:

> *Suddenly on looking up from the dusty ground I*
> *perceived in the now brilliant moonlight, and*

casting shadows appropriate to their positions.
three-storied houses of various shapes and sizes
lining both sides of the road.

The scene developed further as the ground became cobblestoned and muddy. His wife pointed and in shock described the same scene. Sanderson was convinced the buildings were Parisian. After marveling at them for some time, the couple began to feel very dizzy. Sanderson called out, to the assistant, who was some distance ahead. The man turned back and the biologist begged him for a cigarette. As the flame from the assistant's lighter was extinguished, so was the scene from fifteenth century France. Furthermore, the assistant had been oblivious of the vision and had noticed nothing unusual.

In 1973, a coin collector from Norfolk, England not only claimed to have slipped back in time, but produced physical evidence to back this up. A fellow numismatist told him of a shop in Great Yarmouth which sold small plastic envelopes ideal for holding single coins. He had a general idea of the shop's location and found the likely place in a cobbled street.

Inside, the shop was incredibly old-fashioned. The young female assistant added to the atmosphere of a former age. She wore a long black skirt and a blouse with leg-of-mutton sleeves, and her hair was piled on top in a bun.

The customer asked for the small envelopes and the girl turned to a box containing a large number of the objects. He remarked on this, considering their scarcity, and she told him that men from the sailing ships bought them for their fish hooks. He was charged a "shilling" for the envelopes.

He returned a week later for further envelopes but discovered the cobbles had now gone and the decor and interior of the shop. changed. A mature female assistant denied any knowledge of the young girl and replied that they did not stock the small plastic envelopes. The manager backed up her statement. Fortunately, the customer still had the original envelopes. They had been placed in a paper bag with the shop's name printed on it, but after a few days the bag had fallen into bits and was burnt. The envelopes also aged quickly, turning brown and becoming brittle.

Another British case of a time slip took place in Leeds Castle in Kent. Alice Pollock was experimenting by touching objects in Henry VIII's room in an attempt to experience events from another time. After a period of receiving no impressions whatsoever, the room suddenly changed. It lost its modern, comfortable appearance to become cold and bare. The carpet had disappeared and there were now logs burning on the fire. A tall woman in a white dress was walking up and down the room; her face seemed to be in deep concentration. Not long after, the room returned to its original state.

Later research found that the rooms had been the prison of Queen Joan of Navarre, who had been accused of witchcraft by her husband.

In summarizing time slips, the following have been noted:

- The absence of natural sounds, such as a bird song and traffic noises at the onset of a time slip.

- Time slips seem to require a "trigger." This could be a sudden bright light, or abnormal amounts of electrical energy in the atmosphere which if conditions are exactly right, interact with the brain of a percipient.

- Time-slip percipients often report the sensation of existing in two time zones simultaneously - one overlapping the other.

- Our physical selves operate in the three dimensions of space only, but consciousness moves forwards and backwards through time.

- Time slips are not imaginary constructs. Often the information is discovered to be entirely accurate.

CHAPTER 4

Invisibility Cases - Now You See Them, Now You Don't

Over the years a small percentage of my patients have reported instances in their lives in which they become invisible! These examples include waiting on line in a supermarket, bank or department store, when suddenly they are completely ignored by others. In these cases the individual is physically still there, but unable to be seen or even heard. The invisible subject can't understand this because the world appears perfectly normal to them. These encounters usually last for no longer than 10 minutes. My research has shown that these cases are examples of teleportation.

We can trace ancient reports of human invisibility to the Indian *Vedas* (1000 B.C.) and *Upanishads* (700-300 B.C.), which describe *siddhas*, or supernormal abilities including invisibility, as a result of spiritual growth.

Shamans from all over the world, tribes in the polar region and the Aborigines of Australia report such cases of human invisibility. The Rosicrucians tell of the use of clouds, or bodies of mist to create invisibility.

This cloud could, very well be dark matter, which is unionized and therefore invisible to the naked eye. Scientists estimate that between 90 to 95 percent of our universe is composed of this dark matter. Our soul and the other dimensions (astral, causal, mental, etheric and soul plane) are made up of this dark matter.

Theoretically, science tells us that unionized clouds or matter will absorb all light entering it, preventing waves from being refracted or reflected and thus not allowing these light waves from passing through an individual. The result is invisibility.

Traveling in the fifth dimension uses this mechanism. This is how a time traveler from our future (chrononauts) can interact with us and remain invisible, as I detail in my book *Time Travelers from Our Future*. Let us not forget the invisibility reports of many UFO abductees.

The invisibility reports I have received come from patients, who are well educated and adjusted, possess a higher degree of psychic powers and are completely shocked at their temporary invisibility. This phenomena is most definitely not faked or used to gain attention (secondary gain). Also, any clothes and jewelry are equally invisible, suggesting the individual actually teleports into the fifth dimension.

Vanishment Cases

These are cases in which people, or objects, have suddenly vanished. They can only be explained as examples of teleportation.

On November 10, 1939, during the Sino-Japanese War, 3,000 men commanded by Chinese Colonel Li Fu Sien disappeared completely. Their radio ceased transmitting, and all that was found were a few weapons. No Japanese records show the capture of an entire Chinese regiment at that time, and any mass desertion would have been known to their families.

A U.S. steamship, the *Iron Mountain*, disappeared in 1872 on the Mississippi River. It was nearly 200 feet long and thirty feet wide. No trace of this ship or its fifty-five passengers and crew were ever found.

In New York on December 12, 1829 75 year old chief justice of the New York Supreme Court John Lansing went out in the early evening to mail some letters and was never seen again, despite and extensive search.

In 1809 British diplomat Benjamin Bathurst stopped to have dinner at an inn in the town of Perleberg following a return trip from Hamburg, Germany. Bathurst went to examine the horses of the coach he was about to board. His traveling companion witnessed Bathurst disappearing never to be seen again.

In 1975 Jackson Wright was driving his wife Martha from New Jersey to New York City. Once through the Lincoln Tunnel, Jackson drew up to wipe the windshield while Martha cleared the back window. When he looked round, she had disappeared.

CHAPTER 4

David Lang's Teleportation in Tennessee

On the afternoon of September 23, 1880, in Gallatin, Tennessee, David Lang had just returned from a business trip to Nashville when he suddenly vanished. Both children (Sarah and George) were arguing over toys he had brought them from that trip. Three witnesses (his wife Emma Lang, Judge Peck and Peck's brother-in-law Mr. Wade) observed Lang vanishing in front of his home.

As Lang was crossing the pasture, the horse and buggy of the family's friend, Judge August Peck, came into view on the lane in front of the house. A moment later David Lang completely disappeared in mid-step. All the witnesses ran to the spot they had last seen David, but there was nothing to hide behind or under; the field contained just grass. An extensive search turned up nothing, and the county surveyor stated that bedrock started just a few feet below the surface, so no cave-in could have occurred. The surveyor confirmed that the field was on perfectly solid ground, with no caves or sink holes.

Months after the occurrence, in 1881, Lang's children noticed that the grass at the site of their father's disappearance had grown strange and yellow, and formed a circle with about a fifteen foot diameter. Sarah called to her father, and both the children heard him faintly calling for help, over and over, until his voice faded away.

This circle became quite noticeable as horses refused to walk across it. No living creatures (including insects) could be observed in this circle. Emma Lang died shortly thereafter.

Sarah tried desperately to contact her dead mother and in April 1929 she exhibited automatic writing and received the following message: "Together now and forever...after many years...God bless you." Sarah found a copy of a book her father had given her and located a handwritten note by her father in the front of the book. A handwriting expert subsequently confirmed the fact that that Sarah's automatic writing was written by David Lang.

TELEPORTATION

This is a rare account of a teleportation that resulted in the permanent disappearance of an individual. I have conducted several of these on patients and have teleported myself. It is a harmless, but powerful, experience!

Here is an actual description of teleportation from one of my patients:

> *The first time I teleported it was the strangest experience. The entire trip was characterized by a strange feeling throughout my body. It was as though something twisted my body. It felt almost like I was caught in a giant web. Suddenly the world exploded into countless billions of glowing threads. They stretched away in all directions, and they intersected everything including me.*
>
> *I could now perceive that the strange twisting sensation that I was experiencing as correlated with the motion of these "threads." And they were in constant motion. I could feel the world. I could see the room around me, superimposed within the pattern of these threads. I was also aware of things beyond the room. In fact, it seemed like I was aware of everything, although not in any detail. It's somewhat difficult to explain. The overall effect was very similar to looking at a hologram, except it was visceral as well as visual-you could see/feel the image, but you could also see/feel the interference pattern. The difference was that the "interference pattern" was not flat, but extended in all directions.*
>
> *Part of me was totally confused, and another part of me was completely familiar with whatever this was. There was a very odd sense of my consciousness being split. What I mean by that is that two contradictory thoughts were present in my mind simultaneously.*

These effects disappeared almost immediately upon my arrival at both locations. They became less and less and eventually I became so accustomed to the experience that they nearly disappeared.

Other people have described the following regarding teleportation excursions:

- A rush of heat coupled with exhilaration.

- The air filling up with sparkles.

- A sense of expanding in size.

- A lingering of pleasure and spiritual enhancement.

My Own Teleportation

During the 1980s my office was located in Baltimore, Maryland. It was in late December in 1985 and the weather was quite cold. I had seen one of my local patients on a Friday afternoon and she made an appointment for her out of town cousin visiting for Monday morning.

It was Sunday morning and I longed for warm weather. I was recalling a great vacation I had in Montego Bay , Jamaica several years before. My solution was to teleport there.

I changed into my swimsuit, placed my radio, beach towel and snorkeling goggles by my living room couch and played my teleportation tape. My three dogs (Karma, Phoenix and Alpha) observed this odd behavior for a Sunday morning.

The next things I observed was walking along an isolated part of a beach in Montego Bay. A young, attractive visiting college student was sunbathing and commented on my rapid appearance on this section of the beach. She didn't know how I could have appeared from nowhere.

I spent several hours swimming and sunbathing. My new friend and asked me how long I would be in town. I informed her that this was my last day in the Caribbean.

Suddenly, I returned to my living room couch with a puzzled look from all three of my dogs. My bathing suit was wet, there was sand in my sneakers and, most interesting, I had a suntan. The only logical explanation was teleportation.

When my new patient arrived on Monday morning she commented on how healthy I looked with my tanned face. She assumed I spent the entire weekend in Florida. My explanation to her resulted in a most strange look. Teleportation has that effect on the average person.

Try this visualization method to prepare your mind for teleportation:

>Take a deep breath, fill your chest, and hold it until I tell you to Let Go. I am going to count slowly up to 5 and as I do so, you will take five very deep breaths. And with each deep breath that you take, each time you breath out, you will become more and more relaxed and your trance will become deeper and deeper...breathe deeply...more and more deeply relaxed...deeper and deeper into relaxation...breathe deeper, deeper and deeper relaxed...becoming deeper and deeper in hypnosis. Breathing even more deeply...more and more deep relaxed...more and more deeply relaxed...very, very deep breath....deeper and deeper relaxed...your trance depth is becoming even deeper and deeper...very, very deep breath...very, very deeply relaxed...very, very deeply relaxed.

>Once again, I want you to take one very deep breath...fill your chest...and hold it until I say...Let Go. Then...let your breath out as

quickly as possible...and as you do so...you will feel yourself sagging limply back into the chair and you will become twice as deeply relaxed as you are now...twice deeply relaxed. Now, take that very deep breath...fill your chest...hold it...(15 seconds pause) hold it...(20 to 30 seconds pause) Let go.

- Sit in a comfortable chair facing a bare wall.

- Place a simple object directly in front of your line of vision.

- Stare at this object until you are certain of its color, design, shape and contours.

- Close your eyes and visualize both the object and the room. Recreate all aspects of the room and the location of this object in your mind's eye.

- See this object as if you could look through your closed eyes with X-ray vision. Do not open up you eyes until this image of the object and the room fades.

- Repeat this process two more times.

Alright now. Sleep now and rest. You did very, very well. Listen very carefully. I'm going to count forward now from 1 to 5. When I reach the count of 5 you will be back in the present, you will be able to remember everything you experienced and re-experienced You'll feel very relaxed, refreshed and be able to do whatever you have planned for the rest of the day or

evening. You'll feel very positive about what you've experienced and very motivated about your confidence and ability to play this tape again, to improve your ability to visualize and prepare yourself for teleportation. Alright now. 1 very, very deep. 2, you're getting a little bit lighter, 3, you re getting much, much lighter, 4, very, very light, 5, awaken. Wide awake and refreshed.

This next exercise trains you in the art of transferring your consciousness safely into an inanimate object. Before trying this approach place a glass across the room in which you are located:

Now listen very carefully. I want you to imagine a brilliant white light coming down from above and entering the top of your head, filling your entire body. See it, feel it. and it becomes reality. Now imagine an aura of pure white light emanating from your heart region, again surrounding your entire body, protecting you. See it, feel it and it becomes reality. Now only your Higher Self, Masters and Guides and highly evolved loving entities who mean you well will be able to influence you during this or any other hypnotic session. You are totally protected by this aura of pure white light.

In a few moments, I am going to count from 1 to 20. As I do so you will feel yourself rising up to the superconscious mind level where you will be able to receive information from your Higher Self. Number 1, rising up. 2, 3, 4, rising higher. 5, 6, 7, letting information flow. 8, 9, 10, you are halfway there. 11, 12, 13, feeling yourself rising even higher. 14, 15, 16, almost there. 17, 18, 19, number 20.

Now you are there. Take a moment and orient yourself to the superconscious mind level.

PLAY NEW AGE MUSIC FOR 1 MINUTE. [*]

You are now in a deep hypnotic trance and from this superconscious mind level, you are in complete control and able to access this limitless power of your superconscious mind. I want you to be open and flow with this experience. You are always protected by the white light.

Now open your eyes and focus your concentration on the glass across the room. Try to merge with this glass. Continue with this exercise until you are one with the glass and experience yourself in the glass.

PLAY NEW AGE MUSIC FOR 2 MINUTES.

Now try projecting your soul across a room and think from that perspective. Do not visualize or lift out or separate the astral body from your physical one.

PLAY NEW AGE MUSIC FOR 2 MINUTES.

End this Procedure by simply willing your consciousness back to your physical body.

Now practice projecting your consciousness far away from your physical body. This step begins much like the previous step, but now visualize your physical body dematerializing

---

[*]   Dr. Goldberg's website has New Age music for these exercises.

and traveling at least several miles away by concentrating on a person or location.

PLAY NEW AGE MUSIC FOR 2 MINUTES.

Terminate his step by simply visualizing your physical body rematerializing in your original location. Alright now. Sleep now and rest. You did very, very well. Listen very carefully. I'm going to count forward now from 1-5. When I reach the count of 5 you will be back in the present, you will be able to remember everything you experienced and re-experienced. You'll feel very relaxed, refreshed and you'll be able to do whatever you have planned for the rest of the day or evening. You'll feel very positive about what you've experienced and very motivated about your confidence and ability to play this tape again, to condition your mind for teleportation. Alright now. 1, very, very deep. 2, you're getting a little bit lighter, 3 you're getting much, much lighter, 4, very, very light, 5, awaken. Wide awake and refreshed.

This next exercise deals with teleporting to visit a friend. Precede this script with my standard white light protection:

Visualize the face of the person to visit. See only the face and try to see it in clearest detail. As you hold this image in your mind's eye, you will at first begin to remember the clothes the person wore, how they acted, what they said and did, but pay no attention to these recollections.

Simply focus in on the face, not the body or actions and gradually these impressions will begin to fade. As they do, you may pick up a tiny spot of light, or maybe large one, somewhere away from the face but definitely in your line of vision. Try to focus in on it. Usually it will seem fairly close to you, almost as if it were suspended in midair about ten to twelve inches from your eyes. When you perceive this "intruder" your otherwise clear picture of the face of the person you are trying to reach, concentrate upon it. You will find that it will appear to expand and include more detail. As this grows, notice the small spot expanding until it becomes a definite location like a room, or an automobile, or stadium, and in this location you will see the person you are trying to reach. See them as they actually are and in their exact surroundings at that precise moment. Remember, you cannot bring this in by force of will. Once you see the other person's face clearly, relax a little. Try to be passive rather than active. You are trying to receive an impression, not create one. So let it come in. Stay here as long as you feel comfortable before returning to your practice room and ending this trance.

This exercise is a true teleportation technique, and should be practiced only upon mastering the previous methods:

Now I want you to concentrate on the muscle groups that I point out to you. Loosen them, relax them while visualizing them. You will notice that you may be tense in certain areas and limp. And now as you feel the muscles relaxing, you will notice that you begin to feel heavy and relaxed and tired all over your body begins to feel v-e-r-y, v-e-r-y tired and you are going to feel d-r-o-w-s-i-e-r and d-r-o-w-s-i e-r, from the top of your head right down to your toes. Every breath you take is going to soak in deeper and deeper and deeper, and you feel your body getting drowsier and drowsier.

Now listen very carefully. I want you to imagine a bright white light coming down from above and entering the top of your head, filling your entire body. See it, feel it and it becomes reality. Now imagine an aura of pure white light emanating from your heart region, again surrounding your entire body, protecting you. See it, feel it and it becomes reality. Now only your Higher Self, Masters and Guides and highly evolved loving entities who mean you well will be able to influence you during this or any other hypnotic session. You are totally protected by this aura of pure white light.

In a few moments, I am going to count from 1 to 20. As I do so you will feel yourself rising up to the superconscious mind level where you will be able to receive information from your Higher Self. Number 1, rising up. 2, 3, 4, rising higher. 5, 6, 7, letting information flow. 8, 9, 10, you are halfway there. 11, 12, 13, feeling yourself rising even higher. 14, 15, 16, almost there. 17, 18, 19, number 20. Now you are there. Take a moment and orient yourself to the superconscious mind level.

PLAY NEW AGE MUSIC FOR 1 MINUTE.

You are now in a deep hypnotic trance and from this superconcious mind level, you are in complete control and able to access this limitless power of your superconscious mind. I want you to be open and flow with this experience. You are always protected by the white light.

At this time I would like you to ask your Higher Self to assist you in the teleportation of your physical body. Trust your Higher Self and your own ability to allow any thoughts, feelings or impressions that come into your subconscious mind concerning this goal. Do this now.

Allow all outside thoughts during this relaxation phase to drift passively through your mind. Suggest to yourself that at any time you may experience a teleportation and this projection would be terminated if your physical body felt in any way uncomfortable. You may begin to detect a faint "pop" sound in one ear. This indicates you are about to teleport your physical body. Choose a destination (or person) where you wish to visit and focus on this location or individual. Use your five senses, at this time; see the colors, smell the flowers, etc. If you are having trouble with visualization, merely think about this destination or acquaintance.

Shortly, you will find yourself standing in the center of this scene. Wherever you place your thoughts, your physical body is bound to follow. Be wary of your thoughts at this time, as each cognition may direct the physical body to return to your present location instantly. To return to your original site, all you need to do is think about it and that will be accomplished instantaneously. Let yourself now experience an actual teleportation.

This exercise is presented in my Time Travelers Training Program CD Album, which instructs you to explore the fifth dimension, meet time travelers from our future and teleport your physical body anywhere on this planet and to other dimensions safely and return to your present location. Other fifth dimension exercises, including OBE training, are available from my website (www.drbrucegoldberg.com), check out the *Astral Voyage* CD Album for the OBE self-hypnosis CDs.

CHAPTER 5

OUT-OF-BODY TRAVEL

OUR MULTIDIMENSIONAL UNIVERSE

Although the history of society has been fraught with repression, slavery, corruption, wars and other types of human perversion, humankind has never lost sight of the fact that we live in a multidimensional universe.

We have always had the benefit of Masters attempting to remind us of the wisdom of the ancients. For example, consider the techniques of Zoroaster, Confucius, Lao-Tze, Mohammed, Buddha, Moses and Jesus. Most of our knowledge of the other dimensions have originated from the East, especially India.

Our soul (subconscious mind) is electromagnetic energy and exists in equilibrium with other dimensional fields within the space-time continuum. In our universe there are two types of dimensions or planes. The lower five planes consist of the physical, astral, causal, mental and etheric. We draw upon certain subtle bodies representing each of these dimensions to access higher knowledge, recharge our various bodies energy source and provide a mechanism for our soul to grow spiritually by its purification. All of this is supervised by our Higher Self.

When we cross into spirit (clinically die) on any of these dimensions, our destination is the soul plane (a type of demilitarized zone that is neither a lower or higher plane), from which we select our next lifetime or ascend to the higher planes to join God.

We cannot ascend until all of our karmic lessons are learned and our soul is perfect. The soul plane is the last dimension in which we possess any type of body. There are seven higher planes, the higher of which is called the God or nameless plane, that represents the eternal now. There is no cause and effect, no evil, no perpetrators or victims and no time as we know it on the higher planes. All that exists is bliss and love.

The following chart summarizes each of these thirteen dimensions and their characteristic sounds:

Name of Plane	God	Description
13. God or nameless plane	Characteristic Sounds	The true Heaven or Nirvana
12. 11. 10. 9. 8. 7.	Indescribable orchestra-like music is heard continually representing the sounds of the universe	The details of these planes can only be ascertained when you have perfected your soul's energy and have ascended. There is no time, space or cause and effect here. Souls occupying eternity do not possess a body of any kind. They are all perfect energy.

6.	Single note of a flute	This is where each soul goes following death on the lower planes to choose their next life. Beyond this plane there is no body of any type. Self-realization and ascension occurs here.
5.	Buzzing of Bees	The source of the subconscious.
4.	Running Water	The source of moral teachings, ethics and philosophy of the God of the most orthodox religions.
3.	Tinkle of Bells	Akashic records are kept here.
2.	Roar of the Sea	The source of emotions and all psychic phenomena. All ideas concerning physical plane inventions originate here.
1.	Thunder	Illusion of reality the plane of space, time, matter and energy.

The Astral Plane is much larger than its physical counterpart, and its borders extend literally thousands of miles above its surface. This dimension is what physicists seem to refer to as the fifth dimension, for all past, present, and future events occur simultaneously on the Astral Plane. Every material object and particle on the physical plane has an astral counterpart, composed of astral matter.

Entities on the astral plane are conscious only of objects on their dimension. They cannot see physical matter from our plane. However, an astral inhabitant may use a medium or attach itself to the aura of a resident of the physical plane, and thereby gain access to our world.

Another oddity of the astral plane is the Astral Light. This is a vehicle that assists in the movement of beings on that dimension. This Light also has access to the Akashic records (stored on the causal plane), analogous to a computer terminal tapping into a mainframe.

Animals have souls too, so their astral counterparts are present on the Astral Plane. Every monster we have seen in a film, ghost-like character, cartoon figure, and representatives of any and all of our thoughts, desires, and emotions will be present on the Astral Plane.

This includes such nature-spirits as elves, pixies, trolls, satyrs, fauns, imps, goblins, fairies, and so on. All types of thought-forms become a reality on the Astral Plane, even though their presence on the physical plane is temporary. Occultists used the term "elemental" to refer to these thought-forms. These manifestations of our love, kindness, jealousy, insecurity, and evil thoughts and emotions give rise to an entity on the Astral Plane.

When spirits are in the normal conditions of astral life, they appear as glimmering lights. When they wish to manifest themselves to mortals, they assume (in order to be recognized) the physical appearance similar, but often much younger, to that they had in their physical body. They may also appear quite different from their earthly form. When viewed from a distance, their normal appearance is that of small blue lights. These astral inhabitants look like a round blue object up close. The astral body may appear much younger than the biological and chronological age of the physical body, especially when observed in a mirror.

Astral bodies may look ovoid in form within an egg-shaped envelope. They are larger and taller than the physical body. They may also appear luminous and give off a glow that can illuminate a completely darkened room.

The astral body will be dressed in clothes associated with something that the projector is thinking about, or an event that occurred in the past. Garments may be an exact replica of current clothes worn by the voyager, or an improved version of it.

Since our astral body is associated with sensation, passion, and other intense emotions, it is continually altering its appearance to reflect our current emotional state. When psychics observe the astral body they may see various colors that reflect our emotional state.

Characteristics of a typical astral voyage include:

- The physical body becomes immobile and rigid (this effect can be neutralized by white light protection and other techniques in my tapes). The voyager is unable to move his or her limbs. This response ends once the two bodies separate.

- A pulsating silver cord connects the astral body to the physical body. This cord appears to become thinner as the distance between the two bodies increases.

- The astral body is weightless, but possesses very acute perceptive abilities, especially toward sounds and bright and vivid colors.

- It is the physical body that now appears as an empty shell. The focal point of consciousness is from the astral body.

- Awareness of being out-of-body is usually due to the inability to move objects on the physical plane.

- We see some portion of the environment that could not possibly be perceived from where our physical body is known to be at the time.

- We know at the time that we are not dreaming or experiencing a fantasy. Although we may deduce that this cannot be happening, we are in possession of all of our critical functions and later can state with absolute certainty that the astral voyage was not a dream.

- Voyagers commonly describe a sensation of moving through a dark tunnel and entering a white light.

- The senses of perception are more acute in this new dimension.

- The soul commonly leaves the physical body at the solar plexus or stomach area for those individuals who are relative novices at astral voyaging. When you become more adept at leaving the body, other exit points are: the third eye region between the eyebrows, the back of the head, the heart chakra, and the 7th chakra, located at the top of the head (some studies report this as the most common exit point).

- When beyond the physical body, there are no physical laws as we know on the Earth plane. All time is simultaneous, so that you can view any past, present, or future activity on the physical plane.
- The presence of spirit guides, other departed souls and fellow astral voyagers are reported.

- Distances are traveled at the speed of light. All the astral body has to do (when properly trained) is think of a location and arrive there in an instant.

- Some astral voyagers remain in the same location with the physical body, while others travel thousands of miles away.

- Sensations of "tugging" at the back of the head are felt when the OBE is too long in duration. This precedes the return to the physical body.

- A common fear is that the unattended physical body will die - the most common trigger for the astral body to reunite with its physical counterpart. A loud noise can also bring about the end of this metaphysical sojourn. This final step occurs in an instant.

IBES

Years ago I coined the term IBE, which stands for in-the-body experiences. All of the characteristics an OBE are present, except the soul is still in the physical body and not in the corner of the room viewing its physical counterpart. When you have an IBE, you can see and hear into the fifth dimension, but your perspective is still from the vantage of the physical body. The main advantage of an IBE is that it can easily result in an OBE.

Common characteristics reported by OBE subjects include:

- Sensations of leaving and re-entering the physical body.

- The experience of dual consciousness when near the physical body.

- Colors are perceived more vividly, as are objects.

- Scenes of unexplainable beauty are noted. These are often unrelated to the physical environment.

- Feelings of "tuggings" at the back of the head when the OBE is too long in duration. This precedes the return to the physical body.

- The astral world is usually somewhat different from the physical world.

The study of OBE has emerged from its anecdotal beginnings to the domain of scientific experimentation. OBE research demonstrates that it is possible for consciousness to exist apart from the physical body. This suggests that consciousness could indeed survive death.

Various examples of healing are reported during these OBE states. The basic principles of OBE healing are:

- Because healing energies originate at a spiritual level, they can work on any facet of a person's being.

- The patient must be motivated and willing to experience OBE healing. Each one of us has free will to accept or reject healing energies.

- The Higher Self directs the union of the patient and OBE healer by way of energy.

- Illness is not seen as a problem to be fought against. It is a condition of imbalance of energies. The purpose of illness is to bring something to our attention.

- OBE healing cooperates with the body's own healing forces rather than overriding them.

- OBE healing is completely natural and every one of us has the ability to draw up this healing energy resource.

Characteristics of People Who Exhibit OBEs

- They are more empowered and look at the opposites of life as being meaningfully related.

- They keep intense emotions separate and sealed off from their traditional behavior.

- They are more creative, more sensitive to criticism and demonstrate higher levels of intense thoughts and feelings.

- They have a much lower fear of death. We must bear in mind that the OBE mechanism is critical to reincarnation and ascension.

- Their electroencephalograph (EEG) readings exhibit greater synchronization between their left and right brains.

- Approximately twenty percent exhibited their first OBEs during severe physical illness, childbirth, drug use (including general anesthetics), or extreme states of physical or psychological threats.

- During an OBE their skin may appear very dry and warm to the touch. Their brain waves (EEG) tend to exhibit a narrow frequency band and produce visible distortions of the body, along with a deep state of physical relaxation. The body appears more comatose than asleep. There is always a slowing down of the brain waves and a shifting of energy focus. **There has never been physical, psychological harm or death associated with an OBE.**

I personally have been out-of-the-body over 1,000 times with no ill effects.

Helpful Hints for OBEs

1. Desire is always the key. Before going to sleep tell yourself that you are going to remember your OBEs during the dream state.

2. Say to yourself you are going to have conscious recall of your OBE attempts during the day and repeat this often.

3. Always be alone and in a quiet and comfortable environment when you practice OBE.

4. Relaxation is they key. Lay on your back in total comfort making certain you have no tight clothing, heavy bedding or other distracting constraints on your body.

5. Deep breathing. Breathe deeply and rhythmically. It is as important to exhale as to inhale. Breathe in a state of relaxation. Your deep breathing will cause your physical body to vibrate and attune to the astral body.

6. Choose a target. Select a location on this dimension or any other dimension and describe it to yourself. Then request assistance from the universe to travel there.

7. Allow your body to vibrate. While breathing deeply and relaxed, your body will begin to vibrate. Allow this process to happen gradually and as you become more accustomed to it until all the muscles and bones of your body are vibrating. Then tell your astral body to project.

The reason these other dimensions are invisible to our eyes and scientific equipment is because they vibrate at a higher frequency than our universe. Doorways to these dimensions exist both inside and outside the human mind.

When the astral body begins to separate from its physical counterpart a tingling sensation is often felt in the stomach, chest and solar plexus areas of our physical body. The astral body always appears younger, taller, thinner and more attractive than our physical body. Animals leave their body regularly, especially pets.

Although our soul leaves the physical body during an OBE, a copy of its consciousness and memory stays with the physical body. You need not be concerned about an unprotected physical body during your OBEs, nor should you worry about being possessed by a lower astral entity.

Many voyagers report a "click" or "pop" sound at the moment of separation. A sitting position is best for OBEs, both for ease of separation of the astral body and recall of the experience. Always keep your eyes closed during projection attempts.

Metal objects (especially jewelry) interfere with projection attempts. It is best to have your head north if you are lying down. The week of the full moon facilitates OBEs. If you want to meet specific people in the fifth dimension, the better you know this individual the more likely you are to be able to reach them.

Briefly looking at your hands and then looking away again helps to stabilize a projection. Staring at a shiny metal object is also recommended.

Many astral voyagers describe the astral plane from above it as a combination vertical and horizontal grid lines giving it a somewhat checkered appearance over its surface. Brilliant multicolored geometric designs are also reported.

Some first-time projectors describe a feeling of immobility and rigidity, leading to frustration in not being able to control their physical body. This feeling decreases once separation of the two bodies is complete. A blackout is experienced at the precise moment of separation. The silver cord is visible. In the initial voyage, the weightless astral double has very acute powers of perception (hyperthesia). Bright; vivid colors and unusual sounds are detected. Dual consciousness is exhibited, with the astral body being the real self and the physical body now viewed as a shell.

Most beginning astral travelers can pass through physical objects, but are unable to touch or move them. They usually discover that travel is at lightning speed. Most initial voyages end due to fear of danger to the physical body. This unwarranted concern results in an instantaneous return to the physical state. This initial experience is considered very enjoyable, and most voyagers want to have many more of these fifth dimensional trips.

The Silver Cord

Fifth dimensional voyagers describe a silver cord that attaches the astral body to its etheric counterpart. A pulsating silver cord most commonly is connected from the forehead (or sometimes the solar plexus or stomach area) of the etheric body to the back of the astral head.

We do not see this cord when out of the body unless we turn around and look back. My patients have .described this attachment as a tape, thread, ribbon, or an umbilical cord. This last description is most accurate; it is theorized that all the learning and spiritual advances our astral body make are fed back into our physical body through this silver cord.

The majority of descriptions state that this cord is about two or three inches thick when within ten feet of the physical body. It pulsates (I feel it is our consciousness that creates this pulsating, and that it thins out as the astral body distances itself from the physical.) This connection is always maintained until the death of the physical body. Even near-death experiencers describe this attached silver cord.

I believe the mental, spiritual, and physical nourishment that is transmitted along this silver cord to the physical body makes it function much like the umbilical cord of a developing fetus. This silver cord is probably also responsible for our sharpened senses when astral voyaging.

One reason it is nearly impossible to examine your physical body closely while astral voyaging relates to the pulsating silver cord connecting the two bodies. This cord creates a light pulling or tugging sensation throughout the projection. The closer you get to your physical body, the greater this pull becomes.

There is a critical point, usually just a few feet from the physical body, where the cord's pull suddenly brings the astral body back into its physical counterpart. I have had this experience several dozen times myself.

The Five Stages of Astral Projection

Although each individual will have a somewhat unique experience, there are certain commonalities to astral voyaging. They can be described as five separate stages.

Stage One

The sleep state is characterized by the astral body moving out of alignment with its physical counterpart. This allows for a comprehensive recharging of both the astral and mental bodies, as the physical body attains its nightly rest. We leave our body every night during the sleep cycle (especially in the dream or REM phase).This stage can also be exhibited when we are fully conscious(see my OBE example in Florida).

Stage Two

This stage is characterized by the astral body being projected several feet away from its physical body. Often this is noted as a result of an accident or trauma. The projector leaves his or her body to avoid pain, and watches others attending to its physical counterpart from a distance. Joggers running long distances report this type of OBE.

Stage Three

The astral double in this stage is sent several hundred or thousand feet away, but always within familiar surroundings. You can travel to a target of your desire at this time. The occult law, "Energy follows thought" applies here. A strong-enough desire to be with a loved one or a special place can result in the astral body traveling great distances.

CHAPTER 5

Stage Four

The distance traveled by the astral body is rather significant in this stage. Since the astral double can travel at the speed of light, it arrives instantly at most destinations. The distance traveled is directly proportional to the desire and will of the astral body.

Stage Five

Spiritual growth at its highest level is a characteristic of the fifth stage. Our Masters or Guides or our Higher Self, is with our soul at this phase. Some may refer to these perfect entities as angels, but the role is the same. Voyaging now takes on new meaning, as enlightenment is the main goal.

My Own OBE While Driving

My own trip into the future while driving to Ft. Lauderdale, Florida from the University of Maryland School of Dentistry when a student there back in the early 1970s. Since Christmas vacation represented the only significant break until the summer, I looked forward to these trips. My method of maximizing this vacation time consisted of driving straight to Florida from Baltimore, stopping only four times for gas on the 1,000 mile trip. This particular trip was significant because, while driving in the very early hours of the morning, I nearly dozed off on the highway. Occasionally, a jolting sensation sharpened my conscious awareness.

The next thing I was aware of was arriving in Florida, renting a room in a private residence and being frustrated at not being able to fall asleep due to my now-alert mind. I noticed an unusual design to the wallpaper in the room as I lay on the bed trying to provide my fatigued body with its needed rest. I did eventually fall asleep.

Back on the highway, I was jolted back into a hyper-alert consciousness and completed my trip to Florida. My first thought was, "Did I dream that scene or did I really go into the future?" The difference between this being a mere dream or a teleportation into the future occurred several hours later.

Upon arrival in Ft. Lauderdale every detail of my "dream" manifested into reality. When I purchased a paper, I haphazardly called the telephone number from an ad showing a room to rent in a private home. After arriving at this house I dragged my fatigued body to the bed and found it difficult to sleep, since my mind was still in a hyper-alert state. Lastly, I noticed the wallpaper of the bedroom baring the exact unusual design I had seen on the highway in Georgia several hours before! I had never been to this house before.

My explanation for this event consists of two important principles. First, I did literally see into the future and remained on that same parallel universe or frequency.

Second, this experience most likely was an out-of-body experience or astral projection, since my landlord did not appear to recognize me the "second" time he saw me.

Sanctuary Induction

This is a simple exercise in which you are creating a place in the fifth dimension to attract your Higher Self, Spirit Guides, fellow dimensional travelers, etc. to orient to this exciting realm. My *Encounter the Goddess* CD contains this technique and can be ordered from my website.

> **Sit back, relax, breathe deeply, and send a warm feeling into your toes and feet. Let this feeling break up any strain or tension, and as you exhale let the tension drain away. Breathe deeply and send this warm feeling into your ankles. It will break up any strain or tension, and as you exhale let the tension drain away.**

Breathe deeply and-send this feeling into your knees, let .it break - up any strain or tension there, and as you exhale let the tension drain away. Send this warm sensation into your thighs so any strain or tension is draining away. Breathe deeply and

Send this warm feeling into your abdomen now; all your internal organs are soothed and relaxed and any strain or tension is draining away. Let this energy flow into your chest and breasts; let it soothe you and as you exhale any tension is draining away. Send this energy into your back now. This feeling is breaking up any strain or tension, "and as you exhale the tension is draining away. The deep, relaxing energy is flowing through your back, into each vertebra, as each vertebra assumes its proper alignment. The healing energy is flowing into all your muscles and tendons, and you are relaxed, very fully relaxed. Send this energy into your shoulders and neck; this energy is breaking up any strain or tension and as you exhale the tension is draining away. Your shoulders and neck are fully relaxed. And the deep relaxing energy is flowing into your arms; your upper arms, your elbows, your forearms, your wrists, your hands, your fingers are fully relaxed.

Let this relaxing energy wash up over your throat, and your lips, your jaw, your cheeks are fully relaxed. Send this energy into your face, the muscles around your eyes, your forehead, your scalp are relaxed. Any strain or tension is draining away. You are relaxed, most completely relaxed.

And now float. to your space, leave your physical body and move between dimensions and travel to your space, a meadow, a mountain, a forest, the seashore, wherever your mind is safe and free. Go to that space now. And you are in your space, the space you have created, a space sacred and apart. Here in this space you are free from all tension and in touch with the calm, expansive power within you. Here in this space you have access to spiritual information and energy. Here is the space where you can communicate with your Higher Self. Your flow is in harmony with the flow of the universe. Because you are part of the whole creation you have access to the power of the whole of creation. Here you are pure and free. This is your personal sanctuary.

Stay here for a few minutes and when you are ready let yourself drift up and back to your usual waking reality. You will return relaxed, refreshed, and filled with energy. And you will return now, gently and easily. Open your eyes.

A Hypnotic OBE Exercise

With this added background you are now ready for your initial OBEs. Try this simple hypnotic exercise in a quiet and comfortable practice room.

Let yourself relax completely...and breathe quickly...in...and out. And as you do so you will gradually sink into a deeper, deeper sleep. And as you sink into this deeper, deeper sleep, I want you to concentrate on the sensations you can feel in your left hand and arm. You will feel that your left hand is gradually becoming lighter and lighter. It feels just as though your wrists were tied to a balloon...as if it were gradually pulled up...higher and higher...away from the chair.

It wants to rise up...into the air...toward the ceiling. Let it rise...higher and higher. Just like a cork...floating on water. And, as it floats up...into the air...your whole body feels more and more relaxed...heavier and heavier...and you are slowing sinking into a deeper, deeper sleep.

Your left hand feels even lighter and lighter. Rising up into the air...as if it were being pulled up toward the ceiling. Lighter and lighter...light as a feather. Breathe deeply...and let yourself relax completely. And as your hand gets lighter and lighter...and rises higher and higher into the air...your body is feeling heavier and heavier...and you are falling into a deep, deep sleep.

Now your whole arm, from the shoulder to the wrist, is becoming lighter and lighter. It is leaving the chair...and floating upwards...into the air.

Up it comes...into the air...higher and higher. Let it rise...higher and higher...higher and higher. It is slowly floating up...into the air...and as it does so...you are falling into a deeper, deeper trance.

Visualize a floating sensation spreading throughout your entire body. Continue breathing deeply and feel your soul leaving your body through the top of your head, as it rises up beyond the Earth plane to the astral plane. Note the warm feeling now spreading and permeating throughout your entire body. Allow yourself to receive the guidance and love from your Higher Self and spirit guides.

PLAY NEW AGE MUSIC FOR 2 MINUTES.[*]

Experience a feeling of total love and peace. Let yourself immerse your complete awareness in a sense of balance and centering of your soul's energy.

PLAY NEW AGE MUSIC FOR 4 MINUTES.

Alright now. Sleep now and rest. You did very well. Listen very carefully. I'm going to count forward now from 1 to 5. When I reach the count of 5 you will be back in the body, you will be able to remember everything you experienced and re-experienced, you'll feel very relaxed, refreshed, you'll be able to do whatever you have planned for the rest of the day or evening. You'll feel very positive about what you've just experienced and very motivated about your confidence and ability to play this tape again to experience leaving your physical body safely. Alright now. 1 very, very deep, 2 you're getting a little bit lighter, 3 you're getting much, much lighter, 4 very, very light, 5 awaken. Wide awake and refreshed.

The following OBE hypnotic exercise incorporates a number of different approaches and facilitates your own spiritual growth:

Now listen very carefully. I want you to imagine a bright white light coming down from above and entering the top of your head, filling your entire body. See it, feel it and it becomes

---

[*]   Dr. Goldberg's website has New Age music for these exercises.

reality. Now imagine an aura of pure white light emanating from your heart region. Again surrounding your entire body. Protecting you. See it, feel it and it becomes reality. Now only your Masters and Guides and highly evolved loving entities who mean you well will be able to influence you during this or any other hypnotic session. You are totally protected by this aura of pure white light.

Now focus in on how comfortable and relaxed you are, free of distractions, free from physical and emotional obstacles that prevent you from safely leaving and returning to the physical body. You will perceive and remember all that you encounter during this experience. You will recall in detail when you are physically awake only these matters that will be beneficial to your physical, mental and spiritual being and experience. Now begin to sense the vibrations around you, and in your own mind begin to shape and pull them into a ring around your head. Do this for a few moments now.

PLAY NEW AGE MUSIC FOR 2 MINUTES.

Now as you begin to attract these vibrations into your inner awareness, they begin to sweep throughout your body making it rigid and immobile. You are always in complete control of this experience. Do this now as you perceive yourself rigid and immobile with these vibrations moving along and throughout your entire body.

PLAY NEW AGE MUSIC FOR 3 MINUTES.

You have done very well. Pulse these vibrations. Perceive yourself feeling the pulse of these vibrations throughout your entire awareness. In your own mind's eye, reach out one of your arms and grasp some object that you know is out of normal reach. Feel the object and let your astral hand pass through it. Your mind is using your astral arm, not your physical arm, to feel the object. As you do this you are becoming lighter and lighter and your astral body is beginning to rise up from your physical body. Do this now.

PLAY NEW AGE MUSIC FOR 3 MINUTES.

You've done very well. Now, using other parts of your astral body (your head, feet, chest and back) repeat this exercise and continue to feel lighter and lighter as your astral body begins to rise up from your physical body. Do this now.

PLAY NEW AGE MUSIC FOR 3 MINUTES.

Now think of yourself as becoming lighter and lighter throughout your body. Perceive yourself floating up as your entire astral body lifts up and floats away from your physical body. Concentrate on blackness and remove all fears during this process. Imagine a helium-filled balloon rising and pulling your astral body with it up and away from your' physical body. Do this now.

PLAY NEW AGE MUSIC FOR 3 MINUTES.

Now orient yourself to this new experience. You are out of your body, relaxed, safe and totally protected by the white light. Concentrate on a place, not far away, that you would like to visit with your astral body. Now go to this place. Do this now. Perceive this new environment.

PLAY NEW AGE MUSIC FOR 3 MINUTES.

You've done very well. Now I want you to travel to a destination much farther away. It can be a location across the country or anywhere around the world. Take a few moments and think of this destination and you will be there in a few moments. Do this now.

PLAY NEW AGE MUSIC FOR 3 MINUTES.

Alright now. Sleep now and rest. You did very well. Listen very carefully. I'm going to count forward now from 1 to 5. When I reach the count of 5 you will be back in the body, you will be able to remember everything you experienced and re-experienced, you'll feel very relaxed, refreshed, you'll be able to do whatever you had planned for the rest of the day or evening. You'll feel very positive about what you've just experienced and very motivated about your confidence and ability to play this tape again to experience leaving your physical body safely. Alright now. 1 very, very deep, 2 you're getting a little bit lighter, 3 you're getting much, much lighter, 4 very, very light, 5 awaken. Wide awake and refreshed.

Here is another technique to leave the body that involves visual imagery:

Now listen very carefully. I want you to imagine a bright white light coming down from above and entering the top of your head. Filling your entire body. See it, feel it and it becomes reality. Now imagine an aura of pure white light emanating from your heart region. Again surrounding your entire body. Protecting you. See it, feel it and it becomes reality. Now only your Masters and Guides and highly evolved loving entities who mean you well will be able to influence you during this or any other hypnotic session. You are totally protected by this aura of pure white light.

You are about to embark on an imaginary journey, during which your awareness will be introduced to perceptions that are quite different from anything you have encountered before. You absolutely have the ability to voyage to the astral plane or beyond. Your silver cord will always remain attached to your physical body, protecting you and transmitting communication from your Higher Self to your subconscious.

Continued practice will ensure your success. Your voyages will only be to the upper astral plane or beyond. There is no possibility of ending up on the lower astral plane. Your Higher Self and Masters and Guides are always with you, advising and protecting you. Only positive entities will be a part of this experience.

Now raise your vibrations spreading throughout your body from the bottom of the spine to the top of the head. Feel the vibrations accentuate this ascension. Do this now.

PLAY NEW AGE MUSIC FOR 2 MINUTES.

Your astral body is now separating itself from the physical. See yourself in your mind's eye leave your body through the top of your head. See it happening in your mind and feel it happening in your body.

See your astral body float just about your physical body. As I count forward from 1 to 10, on the count of 10 you will arrive at your upper astral plane destination. 1, 2, 3, moving toward this plane. 4,5, halfway there. 6,7,8, almost there. 9, 10, you are there.

Now begin exploring this dimension at your leisure. Record everything you see, hear, touch, taste and feel in your subconscious, to be remembered later. Do this now.

PLAY NEW AGE MUSIC FOR 3 MINUTES.

Now begin your trip back to the physical plane by first entering a brilliant white light you now see before you. Descend back to your room and merge with your physical body. Note the warm feeling now spreading and permeating throughout your entire body. Stay with this feeling for a few moments.

Experience a feeling of total love and peace. Let yourself immerse your complete awareness in a sense of balance and centering of your soul's energy. Stay with this feeling for a few more moments.

PLAY NEW AGE MUSIC FOR 2 MINUTES.

Alright now. Sleep now and rest. You did very, very well. Listen very carefully. I'm going to count forward now from 1 to 5. When I reach the count of 5, you will be able to remember everything you experienced. You'll feel very relaxed, refreshed, and you'll be able to do whatever you have planned for the rest of the day or evening. You'll feel very positive about what you've just experienced and very motivated about your confidence and ability to play this tape again to voyage to other dimensions. Alright now. 1, very, very deep. 2, you're getting a little bit lighter. 3, you're getting much, much lighter. 4, very, very light. 5, awaken. Wide awake and refreshed.

In this exercise you will be guided out-of-the-body to explore one of the other dimensions in detail:

Now listen very carefully. I want you to imagine a bright white light coming down from above and entering the top of your head. Filling your entire body. See it, feel it and it becomes reality. Now imagine an aura of pure white light emanating from your heart region. Again surrounding your entire body. Protecting you. See it, feel it and it becomes reality. Now only your Masters and Guides and highly evolved loving entities who mean you well will be able to influence you during this or any other hypnotic session. You are totally protected by this aura of pure white light.

Now focus in on how comfortable and relaxed you are, free of distractions, free from physical and emotional obstacles that prevent you from safely leaving and returning to the physical body. You will perceive and remember all that you encounter during this experience. You will recall in detail when you are physically awake only these matters that will be beneficial to your physical and mental being and experience. Now begin to sense the vibrations around you and in your own mind begin to shape and pull them into a ring around your head. Do this for a few moments now.

PLAY NEW AGE MUSIC FOR 2 MINUTES.

Now as you begin to attract these vibrations into your inner awareness, they begin to sweep throughout your body, making it rigid and immobile. You are always in complete control of this experience. Do this now as you perceive yourself rigid and immobile with these vibrations moving along and throughout your entire body.

PLAY NEW AGE MUSIC FOR 3 MINUTES.

You have done very well. Pulse these vibrations. Perceive yourself feeling the pulse of these vibrations throughout your entire awareness.

Feel yourself now able to leave your physical body and travel safely and protected by the white light of your Higher Self to the astral, causal, mental or etheric plane. Your Masters and Guides will also be there for you, assisting you in obtaining the greatest benefit from this experience.

And now going deeper and deeper and deeper, feeling your mind going deeply into trance, feeling your body going deeply into trance, your whole mind-body going deeper, and deeper, as you know and respond to a positive and spiritual force that is greater than any you have known or responded to before for this purpose of deepening trance.

And that force will continue to pull and to draw you, deeper and ever deeper, as now you are becoming very aware of your body, of the form and the substance of your body, and finding yourself now surrounded by darkness, and knowing that your soul's energy has been transported out from your physical body into another dimension.

Your soul is now voyaging to another dimension and taking you deeper and deeper into trance, and toward important new experiences, and liberating within what you have, but in the past could not use. And you will go deeper in order that you may become free.

As I count forward from 1 to 10 you will arrive on the count of 10 at a learning temple on either the astral, causal, mental or etheric plane. If you would like to select a particular plane to visit concentrate on that particular plane now.

Number 1, 2, 3 moving quickly toward this plane. 2,3, 4, 5 you are halfway there. 6,7,8 almost there. 9 and 10 you are there. Take a few minutes and orient yourself to this learning temple. Now you may access your Akashic records and communicate with your Higher Self and/or spirit guides. You may ask any questions about your karmic purpose, past/future life ties with loved ones and anything else you would like to know. Do this now.

PLAY NEW AGE MUSIC FOR 2 MINUTES.

At this time you are free to explore this plane. I want you to take a tour of this dimension accompanied by your Higher Self and perhaps a spirit guide that will describe the components on this plane, and how this experience may assist you in your own spiritual growth. Do this now.

PLAY NEW AGE MUSIC FOR 3 MINUTES.

Alright now. Sleep now and rest. You did very, very well. Listen very carefully. I'm going to count forward now from 1 to 5. When I reach the count of 5 you will be back in your physical body, you will be able to remember everything you experienced and re-experienced, you'll feel very relaxed, refreshed, you'll be able to do whatever you have planned for the rest of the day or evening. You'll feel very positive about what you've just experienced and very motivated about your confidence and ability to play this tape again to experience leaving your physical body safely. Alright now. 1 very, very deep, 2 you're getting a little bit lighter, 3 you're getting much, much lighter, 4 very, very light, 5 awaken. Wide awake and refreshed.

CHAPTER 6

TIME TRAVEL THROUGH THE FIFTH DIMENSION

Although my use of hypnosis functions as a form of time machine - regressing patients to past lives and progressing them to future lives - time travel is not only possible, but can be conceived even with our current knowledge of physics.

I divide time travel into 3 categories. These are:

1. Physical time machines
2. Teleportation
3. Fifth Dimension Travel - Out-of-Body experiences

The first category can best be illustrated by Kip Thorne's enlarging a traversable wormhole paradigm. This research was at the request of the late Carl Sagan, who asked Kip Thorne to research a technically accurate time machine for Sagan's novel *Contact* (which became a feature film starring Jodie Foster).

Theoretically, a wormhole is a time machine that leads to the past or future. By entering a black hole and exiting through a white hole, matter ends up in the future. The reverse also applies.

There are several problems with attempting to use the wormhole to travel through time:

1. Wormholes, as they are theorized to exist in nature, are microscopic.

2. Even if this type of wormhole could be enlarged, a spaceship or human entering it would be crushed by the gravitational "throat" caused by the singularity.

3. As a spaceship crossed the event horizon - the point at which the black hole's gravity becomes so great that light is trapped - the difference in the gravitational pull on different parts of the ship would stretch it, tearing it to pieces.

4. The radiation sucked into the black hole would burn any living creature to vapor.

The solution to this problem is to construct a wormhole that is not associated with black holes or white holes. Einstein showed that this would eliminate the pinching effect. By applying a special "exotic matter" to the sides of this wormhole, it could be made traversable. Exotic matter has negative mass and moves forward in time. This is the exact opposite of anti-matter (electron/positron, for example).

Kip Thorne, Michael Morris, and Ulvi Yurtsever worked on this model and wrote a scientific paper in 1988 published in *Physical Review Letters*[1]. They suggested that the exotic matter should be confined to the central area of the wormhole around the throat and be surrounded by ordinary matter.

Other advantages to using exotic matter are a minimizing of the stretching forces and a tremendous decrease in the radiation levels within this wormhole. Thus exotic matter solves all of the current problems with time travel. The only issue is that we have no such exotic matter today.

Thorne, Morris, and Yurtsever state, "One can imagine an advanced civilization pulling a wormhole out of the quantum foam and enlarging it to classical size." Some interpretations of quantum mechanics suggest that space-time, rather than being a flat void, is made up of a foam-like structure similar to the cellular structure of living beings. This quantum foam is thought by some to contain small wormholes that may be transporting particles back and forth through time. Curved space-time also eliminates the necessity of exceeding the speed of light to travel through time.

Though interpretations vary, there is nothing in the laws of physics as we currently understand them that would rule out the construction of a time machine. Some scientists estimate that we will be able to do so in 500 to 1,000 years.

My research with time travelers ("chrononauts") from 1,000 to 3,000 years in our future, coming back to our time, supports this. These travelers have monitored both our technological and spiritual growth, and I describe their technology and influence on our civilization in my book *Time Travelers from Our Future: A Fifth Dimension Odyssey.* and *Egypt: An Extraterrestrial and Time Traveler Experiment.*

Hugh Everett III is credited with discovering parallel universes while completing his doctoral dissertation in quantum mechanics at Princeton University in 1957. His academic advisor was Martin Kruskal, who created a coordinate map to more fully describe these parallel universes. In Kruskal's map, he traced light as it made its way in and out of a black hole, in the form of coordinate lines.

This gave new meaning to the concept of a black hole. The fact that a black hole led to a white hole gave it a symmetric structure. While we experienced a past event in our universe, this same circumstance appeared as the future for the inhabitants of the parallel universe. Having now established the existence of both a past and future singularity, the black hole functioned like a true time machine, linking two parallel universes and permitting a traveler to move backward or forward in time.

A time machine is represented by this black hole-white hole paradigm, in that the parallel universe we enter into may be our own at an earlier or later date in time. This explains the ability of time travelers to move backward or forward in time without the aid of a physical machine. They could enter this singularity inside one of their vehicles (a flying saucer) and come into our world as a UFO! My research reveals that this mode of time travel will be discovered in about the year 3050 and function through the end of the 34th century.

My research with individuals who have made contact with chrononauts (confirmed by myself utilizing my Fifth Dimension Travel technique) reveals that during the 35th century teleportation will be the mechanism of time travel. This avoids the tear in the fabric of space-time problem and eliminates the need for ships! A time traveler can now simply dematerialize to the 21st century, or anywhere else in time.

This is accomplished by means of a fifth dimensional computer chip-like device contained in a small box they wear. An artist's rendition of a 36th century time traveler named Traksa is pictured on my website (www.drbrucegoldberg.com). He teleports through time and has communicated with me and others in the 21st century.

The third and final method of time travel is through the fifth dimension. This is an out-of-body experience self-hypnosis technique that allows you to go beyond time (the fourth dimension of the space-time continuum) and travel back or forward through time and explore hyperspace. This is the only method of time travel available to us today.

Principles of Time Travel

In voyaging through time there are certain rules and limitations you need to be aware of. Here are some principles that will assist you.

There are only certain time periods and locations you are capable of visiting. Due to your own karmic growth as a soul and so that you don't interfere with the universe's overall plan, some dates and places are beyond your grasp.

It is difficult to specifically go to an exact time, as time travel appears quite sporadic. For example, you may easily move ahead three days in time, but have great difficulty in viewing an occurrence one hour in the future.

These "windows in time" are unique to each individual. Some people find it easy to travel 500 or 1,000 years back or forward in time, but considerably shorter time intervals are out of their reach.

Traveling back in time several hundred years to a scene that takes only a few seconds of time in that bygone era requires perhaps several minutes in the present time frame.

Going into the future by five or six hundred years to an episode that encompasses several weeks in, for example, the twenty-sixth century requires only a few minutes in the present to explore.

Colors appear duller as we voyage back in time. A black-and white monochrome-like effect is commonly observed if we travel great distances back in time.

Traveling into the future results in a sharpening of color perception. The farther ahead in time we travel, the more brilliant these colors appear. Placing ourselves in the twenty-eighth century may very well result in a psychedelic display of colors. This paradigm may also apply to our other senses.

With experience you can control your time traveling to the extent that it can assist your personal or professional life. For instance, these techniques can be used to go into the future by one day to view a business meeting or social date. You not only have the opportunity to overview this exchange, but may be able to maximize your goal because that individual will now feel more comfortable with you, since he or she will have a feeling that they' have met you before.

Always maintain a high code of ethics when using time travel exercises. Never attempt to manipulate others through time travel. Any such unethical motives will be noted by the universe and karmic laws are such that you will lose in the long run.

There is nothing wrong with benefiting materially or in any other way. You may use these techniques to find a soul mate, improve your health, or advance your career. Just refrain from accomplishing these goals at the expense of someone else. "What goes around comes around" is the karmic principle to always bear in mind.

Akashic Records

The Akashic records are a type of chart of all of your past, present, and future lifetimes. They are reportedly kept on the causal plane. These records are what psychics and channelers access when they initiate a reading. We have the capacity to access these records on any plane, but it is easiest to obtain this data on the soul plane. These records accurately reflect our souls growth and what we have yet to learn.

George Noory's Akashic Records

By far my favorite talk show host is George Noory of Premiere Radio Network. He hosts *Coast to Coast AM* on weekdays and we have spent many hours on the air discussing the fifth dimension, Time Travelers, Reincarnation and other related topics. His show is heard on over 500 radio stations with an audience in the millions.

I have discussed my self-hypnosis technique known as Access the Akashic Records to scan both past and future lives of an individual. Prior to one of my interviews with George, I decided to use my technique to see what his future lives would be. Here is a summary of two of George's future incarnations:

Dexter Monterrey - A 22nd Century Radio Host

George's next life takes place in the 22nd century and his name is Dexter Monterrey. Dexter is the host of a radio show on the Global Communications Network (GCN), which has 300 million listeners worldwide. His show is done live in a mall-like complex and you see a hologram of him throughout this structure. All listeners to his show also see a miniature replica of this hologram by their radios, which are sophisticated computers.

His show deals mostly with energy forms of healing and, psychic research (this will be critical to another future life). Dexter is over 6 feet tall with sandy hair, clean shaven, blue eyes and has an athletic physique. He wears a one-piece gold jumpsuit. He is very positive, spiritual and single. He is 40 years old and does this show for over 40 years.

His reputation was built on an exposé he did on "mind pirates"- criminals who use devices to steal ideas from the brains of scientists and inventors to sell on the black market.

He lives in Texas and experiments with OBE travel as a hobby. He never marries and dies of natural causes at age 110.

Xeor - A Psychic Researcher from the 35th Century

During the 35th century teleportation will be the mode of time travel as I discuss in my book *Time Travelers from Our Future*. It is during this century George will be a male psychic researcher named Xeor. Xeor eventually develops a technique of cleansing the soul's aura by way of energy rings (large metal-like brass-like objects) to assist in raising the quality of the soul's energy and removing a form of psychic attack from the lower Astral plane. His research is applied to time travelers in their teleporting back in time, which is relatively new.

Xeor receives much recognition for his work, but is severely attacked by the Black Brotherhood (a lower astral plane hierarchy) just prior to an event held in his honor. Xeor uses his rings to defeat this psychic attack and is even more recognized for his research.

Xeor is a spiritual and modest man who is married to Dilora and has 3 sons who follow him in his research. He lives in Toronto and dies of natural causes at about 800 years old.

We can learn quite a lot about George's karmic purpose from these two future lives. The theme of psychic research (the theme of Dexter Monterrey's show and the profession of Xeor) is present throughout these lifetimes. It is also notable that today George is fascinated by my work with psychic projection and Time Travelers from our future. As Xeor he will be involved with both.

George commented on his future life as Dexter Monterrey in the April, 2009 issue of *After Dark* magazine published by Premiere Radio as follows:

> *Years ago Dr. Bruce Goldberg told me he had accessed the Akashic Records and determined that in the future I would be a celebrity known as Dexter Monterrey. I laughed out loud at the funny name, but as time passed the name grew on me and the whole idea still continues to make me smile.*
>
> *It makes sense that what I learn in this life will leave some sort of cosmic imprint on my soul that allows me to take on a job in communications in the future.*

George is truly a quality soul whom I have come to know well during our many interviews. He is seriously not only interested in this field, but provides an excellent format for the distribution of this knowledge. Thank you my friend for your work and your energy.

Seeing Into the Future

It is rather easy to obtain a glimpse of the future when you use time-tested self-hypnosis techniques. Try this future viewing exercise:

1. **Sit comfortably, apply white light protection and breathe deeply. Visualize a symbol for the future. This may be a radio, book or anything you like. Mentally toss this symbol out into the future and perceive it broadcasting information back to you about your future. Turn your recorder on and verbalize any information you acquire.**

2. **Ask your Higher Self to assist you in this exercise. Now imagine that it is exactly one week from today. See and feel what you are doing. Let any images, thoughts and feelings come into your awareness. What is different about your life at this future date? Record your impressions. Dissolve these images.**

3. **Now perceive it is one month from today. Ask your Higher Self to further help you with this step. What is it exactly that you are planning, doing and thinking? What has changed since the one week information was given to you?**

4. **Follow these same steps and look at three months, six months, one year, and finally five years into your future. Investigate any issues you consider important in your life. Give yourself advice from the perspective of these probable futures.**

5. **Ask your Higher Self to comment on your advice and the accuracy of your probable futures.**

6. **Here are some questions to ask your Higher Self:**

    What can I emphasize in my life during the next week (month, three months, etc) that will facilitate my spiritual growth?

    What specific decisions and choice can I make right now to achieve my highest aspirations?

    What behaviors, thoughts, and actions can I implement to accelerate my spiritual path?

    Think of a current situation in your life and ask, "What am I learning from _____?

    How can I improve my skills as an astral voyager?

    What can I do physically, mentally, emotionally, and spiritually to raise the frequency vibrational rate of my soul?

Here is a script for age progression (viewing the future of your current life). I always recommend making tapes of these techniques. As I stated before, if you would like professionally recorded tapes feel free to contact my office for a comprehensive list of these titles.

Age Progression

Now listen very carefully. I want you to imagine a bright white light, coming down from above and entering the top of your head, filling your entire body. See it, feel it and it becomes reality. Now imagine an aura of pure white light emanating from your heart region, again surrounding your entire body, protecting you. See it, feel it and it becomes a reality. Now only your Higher Self, masters and guides, and highly evolved loving entities who mean you well will be able to influence you during this or any other hypnotic session. You are totally protected by this aura of pure white light. Focus carefully on my voice as your subconscious mind has memories of all past, present and future events.

This tape will help guide you into the future. Shortly I am going to be counting forward from 1 to 20. Near the end of this count you are going to imagine yourself moving through a tunnel. Near the end of this count you will perceive the tunnel veering off to the left and to the right. The right represents the past; the left represents the future.

On the count of 20 you will perceive yourself in the future. Your subconscious and superconscious mind levels have all the knowledge and information that you desire. Carefully and comfortably feel yourself moving into the future with each count from 1 to 20. Listen carefully now. If you have used this technique before and received information about one or more of your other frequencies, I want you to select a different one to explore.

If you have already reviewed your five frequencies and would like to be programmed for your ideal frequency, simply concentrate on the number you have assigned to that ideal frequency and explore that particular path at this time.

Number 1, feel yourself now moving forward to the future, into this very, very deep and dark tunnel. 2, 3 farther and farther and farther into the future. It is a little bit disorienting but you know you're moving into the future. 4, 5, 6, 7, 8, 9 - it's more stable now and you feel comfortable, you feel almost as if you're floating, as you're rising up and into the future. 10, 11, 12 - the tunnel is now getting a little bit lighter and you can perceive a light at the end, another white light just like the white light that is surrounding you. 13, 14, 15 now you are almost there.

Focus carefully. You can perceive in front of you a door to this left tunnel that you are in right now. The door will be opened in just a few moments and you will see yourself in the future. The words "sleep now and rest" will always detach you from any scene you are experiencing and allow you to await further instructions. 16, 17 - it's very bright now and you are putting your hands on the door. 18 - you open the door. 19 - you step into this future, to this future scene. 20 - carefully focus on your surroundings, look around you, see what you perceive.

Can you perceive yourself? Can you perceive other people around you? Focus on the environment. What does it look like? Carefully focus on this. Use your complete objectivity. Block out any information from the past that might have interfered with the quality of the scene. Use only what your subconscious and superconscious mind level will observe. Now take a few moments, focus carefully on the scene, find out where you are and what you are doing, why are you there. Take a few moments; let the scene manifest itself.

PLAY NEW AGE MUSIC FOR 3 MINUTES.[*]

Now focus very carefully on what year this is. Think for a moment. Numbers will appear before your inner eyes. You will have knowledge of the year that you are in right now. Carefully focus on this year and these numbers. They will appear before you. Use this as an example of other information that you are going to obtain. I want you to perceive this scene completely, carry it through to completion. I want you to perceive exactly where you are, who you are, the name, the date, the place. I want you to carry these scenes to completion, follow them through carefully for the next few moments. The scene will become clear and you will perceive the sequence of what exactly is happening to you.

PLAY NEW AGE MUSIC FOR 3 MINUTES.

You've done very well. Now you are going to move to another event. I want you to focus on a difference in the same future time and in the same frequency. Perceive what is going on and why this is important to you. Perceive the year,

---

[*] Dr. Goldberg's website has New Age music for these exercises.

the environment, the presence of others. Let the information flow.

PLAY NEW AGE MUSIC FOR 3 MINUTES.

As you perceive the details of the next scene, also focus in on your purpose. Focus in on what you are learning, what you are unable to learn. Perceive any sequence of events that led up to this situation. Let the information flow surrounding this all-important future event now.

PLAY NEW AGE MUSIC FOR 3 MINUTES.

You have done very well. Now I want you to rise to the superconscious mind level to evaluate this future experience and apply this knowledge to other future frequencies and your current life and situations. 1 rising up. 2 - rising higher. 3 - halfway there. 4 almost there, 5 - you are there. Again, if you have decided that this is your ideal future path and want to be programmed to it, just concentrate on the number you have assigned to it and any significant events that separate it from the other frequencies.

If you are unsure of which is your ideal path, let your Higher Self assist you in making this choice and follow the instructions I previously gave.

Let your Higher Self assist you in making the most, out of this experience. Do this now.

All right now. Sleep and rest. You did very well. Listen very carefully. I'm going to count forward now from 1 to 5. When I reach the count of 5 you will be back in the present,

you will be able to remember everything you experienced and re-experienced. You'll feel very relaxed, refreshed, and you'll be able to do whatever you have planned for the rest of the day or evening. You'll feel positive about what you have just experienced and very motivated about your confidence and ability to play this tape again to experience additional future events. All right now. 1 - very, very deep. 2 - you're getting a little lighter. 3 - you're much, much lighter. 4 - very, very light. 5 - awaken.

This technique of perceiving your different parallel universes and selecting your ideal path is what I term my "New You" approach.

The following represent advantages to using this method and the "New You" technique to your ultimate goal of custom designing your own destiny:

Your confidence in general will increase,. as you find yourself no longer worrying about the outcome of events in your life.

You will receive information and ideas that you could not obtain from your conscious mind proper.

The little successes you initially have increase your motivation for additional applications of this technique, and further add to your self-image.

A feeling of importance is felt, as you now begin to structure your life with specific steps and a timetable. This also means you are assigning an importance to the project of achieving the success and self-fulfillment that you desire.

---

[1]   Kip Thorne, et al. "Wormholes, Time Machines , and the Weak Energy Condition." *Physical Review Letters*, 1988, 61 (13), 1446-1449.

CHAPTER 7

THE TRUTH ABOUT NEAR-DEATH EXPERIENCES

The work of Dr. Raymond Moody, as reflected in his first book *Life After Life*, brought the truth he termed near-death experience (NDE) to the attention of the public. This 1975 book was the result of over eleven years of research on over one hundred and fifty patients.

Moody described a core experience as reported by these patients. This paradigm can be listed as follows:

1. Ineffability
2. Hearing the news of one's own death
3. Feelings of peace and quiet
4. The noise
5. The dark tunnel
6. Out of the body
7. Meeting others
8. The being of light
9. The review
10. The border
11. Coming back[1]

CHAPTER 7

Kenneth Ring, in his book *Life At Death*, describes five categories in the NDE:

1. **The Affective component.** Peace and the sense of well-being. The following responses describing this category appear in Ring's book:

> *I had a feeling of total peace. A feeling of total, total peace ... it was just such a total peaceful sensation - I wasn't frightened anymore. [There was] nothing painful. There was nothing frightening about it. It was just something that I felt I gave myself into completely. And it felt good. ... One very, very strong feeling was that if I could only make them [her doctors] understand how comfortable and how painless it is ... how natural it is ... I felt no sadness. No longing. No fear.*

> *The mellowness and the passiveness that I felt in this state was just so intense ... like I said before, it was a very, very strong - I can only use the words mellow feeling, passive feeling. There wasn't one bit of discontentment that I felt [pause] I can probably say the highest I've ever felt in my life.[2]*

2. **Body separation.** Leaving the body behind. Most NDE reports describe a sense of being separated and detached from their physical body. Their environment is brightly illuminated. Ring gives the following examples:

> *I felt as though I were going to die. The sensation was not painful, but as though I felt a tugging and pulling as in a game of "tug-of-war." Finally, a*

130

'little light hovered over my still form and all my senses were transferred into this small light ..., I, or rather the little light, flew around the operating room watching everything that was taking place.

In another report. Crookall describes a NDE from neither the physical nor astral body:

Sometime during the night, although I was unconscious I saw the hospital room with doctors surrounding Dr. G., who was at my bedside ... At the same time I saw, over my body which was lying on the bed, another body of me suspended in mid-air in the exact position of hanging from the ceiling by what seemed to be a cord attached to my navel. I seemed to be an observer, but from where I cannot say. All I know is that I saw two bodies of myself. I watched this sight for some time.[3]

Osis and Haroldsson give the following account of a sixty-two year old woman's NDE from complications with cancer:

She had a very peculiar look on her face. I rearranged her pillows, slightly elevating her back. She was very lucid. I stepped out of the room. When I came back, her eyes were open, then she had this look on her face, not aware of me, smile, raised right arm as if reaching for something, resting quietly. She seemed to be somewhere else, I can't explain, transposed to another world. I spoke to her, she did not answer. Later she told me that she had heard organ music, saw angels in brilliant white. She was smiling more broadly-very pleased at the whole thing.[4]

3. **Entering the darkness.** This dimensionless phase is accompanied by a sense of floating and rapid movement through space. Many experiencers use the term tunnel to describe this category. As Raymond Moody reports:

> *I had a very bad allergic reaction to a local anesthetic, and I just quit breathing - I had a respiratory arrest. The first thing that happened - it was real quick - was that I went through this dark, black vacuum at super speed. You could compare it to a tunnel, I guess. I felt like I was riding on a roller coaster train at an amusement park, going through this tunnel at a tremendous speed.*[5]

Another patient described his experience as follows:

> *I was in an utterly black, dark void. It was very difficult to explain, but I felt as if I were moving in a vacuum, just through blackness. Yet, I was quite conscious. It was like being in a cylinder which had no air in it. It was a feeling of limbo, of being half-way here, and half-way somewhere else.*[6]

Cardiologist Michael Sabom reports a 23 year old woman's NDE as follows: "There was total blackness around me. I want to say that it felt like I was moving very, very fast in time and space. I was traveling through a tunnel."[7]

4. **Seeing the light.** This light is most often described as a brilliant, golden light. It never hurts the eyes but is very comforting and of indescribable beauty. Sabom cites the following examples:

> *I went through this period of darkness ... There was this light, like someone holding a flashlight, and I started going towards that. And then the whole thing brightened up and the next*

thing I remember was I was floating ... We were going through this shaft of light ... the light kept getting brighter and brighter ... It was so bright, and the closer we got, the brighter it got, and it was blinding.

A 35-year-old survivor of a cardiac arrest told Sabom: "At the end of that tunnel was a glowing light. It looked like an orange glow from the sunset in the afternoon?"[8]

5. **Entering the light.** At this stage, the patient enters into a different world from which the light appears to have come from. This is the most beautiful sight these people have ever encountered. It can take the appearance of many different types of environments. Moody gives the following samples:

I thought I was dead. I looked around and then I was in a tunnel with a bright light at the end. The tunnel seemed to go up and up. I came out on the other side of the tunnel.

There were a lot of people in the light but I didn't know any of them. I told them about the accident and they said I had to go back. They said it wasn't my time to die yet so I had to go back to my father and mother and sister.

I was in the light for a long time. It seemed like a long time. I felt everyone loved me there. Everyone was happy. I feel that the light was God. The tunnel whirled up toward the light like a whirlpool. I didn't know why I was in the tunnel or where I was going. I wanted to get to that light. When I was in the light I didn't want to go back. I almost forgot about my body.[9]

Ring separately describes the decision to return to life, which may very easily be labeled as a sixth category. A panoramic life review is experienced at this time, in the form of a hologram. There are flashbacks and flashforward scenes, with a positive tilt. Often, these patients encounter a presence, which may be a religious figure or their spirit guide. Deceased loved ones may be met also.

Sabom cites some descriptions of this category: "During this stage, my life just flashed in front of my face. My whole life ... Things that had happened to me in my lifetime, like when we got married, just flashed in front of my eyes, flashed and it was gone."[10]

Moody gives a summary of this phenomenon from an English professor:

> *At some point I was shown, or saw, the events of my life. They were in a kind of vast panorama. All of this is really just indescribable. People I know who had died were there with me in the light, a friend who had died in college, my grandfather, and a great aunt, among others. They were happy, beaming.*
>
> *I didn't want to go back, but I was told that I had to by a man in light. I was being told that I had not completed what I had to do in life. I came back into my body with a sudden lurch.*[11]

The truths emanating from these NDE cases show that it represents a distinctive state of consciousness. This transpersonal state completely transforms or removes many common features of cognition and perception. The voice is assumed to be the Higher Self or a spirit guide.

Women are more likely to have an NDE in connection with an illness. NDEs reported by men are more commonly associated with accidents or suicide attempts. Either sex may describe a silver cord that pulsates and connects the astral body to the physical body, usually at the back of the head of the latter. (One has to turn around in this altered state of consciousness to note its presence.)

Attempts by Medicine to Disclaim These Truths

Skeptics point to several biological factors to explain NDEs.

1. **Anesthetics.** The only conceivable way general anesthetics could mimic the core experience would be to elevate the bloods level of carbon dioxide. These drugs actually have no effect on carbon dioxide levels and often the patient is given pure oxygen. CO_2 inhalation will produce a tunnel effect and bright lights. This condition, however, has never produced the Beings of Light or panoramic life review so commonly reported. Furthermore, Dr. Michael Sabom, an Atlanta cardiologist, measured blood oxygen levels on one of his patients at the very instant the patient had a NDE (this was confirmed by the patient's knowledge of instrument readings) and found his oxygen level to be higher than normal.[12] Many NDE receivers had no drugs given to them.

2. **Other drugs.** Hallucinogenic drugs result in a distorted and variable description of the "Trip." As already noted, the core experience in an NDE is clear, real, and fairly consistent.

3. **Temporal lobe stimulation.** Although the panoramic life review may be produced by seizure-like neural firing patterns in the brain's temporal lobe, this does not produce the entire range of effects described in the core experience.

4. **Cerebral anoxia.** NDE reports are not characterized by a cut off of blood flow to the brain. Even if that did happen, a state of unconsciousness would result and the patient would have no memories of this time. Again, the entire range of the core experience would not be exhibited by cerebral anoxia.

5. **Cultural conditioning** from media reports about NDE. Ring's study clearly shows that nearly twice as many of those that had no NDE were aware of this phenomenon and the work of Elisabeth Kübler-Ross and Raymond Moody's work through the media. This defeats any argument that the experiencers were culturally conditioned to have this result. Children also report NDEs but their experiences differ. They have more vivid recalls and see the brilliant white light twice as often as adults. Children have shown the tendency to temporarily forego their childhood identities and become "ageless and wise beyond their years."[13] In addition, the panoramic memory life review is absent in a child's NDE.

Moody reported that a woman was able to accurately describe the instruments that were employed in her resuscitation following a heart attack - right down to their colors.[14] What makes this case especially significant is that this elderly patient had been blind for 50 years!

One rather interesting observation from some NDE reports is that of precognition. Ring reports a "life preview" and "world preview" as a component of these futuristic depictions.[15]

The life previews were glimpses of the patient's future and unique to each individual. However, there was considerable consistency of global events, both in timing and content. The life previews are presented as a vivid memory rather than a forecast and are highly detailed. They seem to occur as an extension of the panoramic life review.

There is documentation to many of these futuristic projections, according to Ring.[16] One man described the Three Mile Island incident to his wife just two days before it happened. Another patient described the eruption of Mt. St. Helens to her husband. He mocked her until a few hours later this event was shown on their local television news.

There are even biblical references to elements characteristic of NDE. The Apostle Paul described the following vision on the road to Damascus:

> *Acts 26:13: At midday, O king, I saw in the way a light from heaven, above the brightness of the sun, shining round about me and them which journeyed with me. And when we were all fallen to the earth, I heard a voice speaking unto me, and saying in the Hebrew tongue, "Saul, Saul, why persecutest thou me? It is hard for thee to kick against the pricks."*

> *And I said, "Who art thou, Lord?" And he said, "I am Jesus, whom thou persecutest. But rise, and stand upon thy feet: for I have appeared unto thee for this purpose, to make thee a minister and a witness, both of these things in which I will appear unto thee..."*

> *"Whereupon, O King Agrippa, I was not disobedient unto the heavenly vision... And as I thus spake for myself, Festus said with a loud voice, "Paul, thou art beside thyself; much learning doth make thee mad."*

> *But I said, "I am not mad, most noble Festus; but speak forth the words of truth and soberness."*

And:

> *1 Corinthians 15:35-52: But some man will say, "How are the dead raised up? And with what body do they come?" Thou fool... (of) that which thou sowest, thou sowest not that body that shall be but bare grain... But God giveth it a body as it had pleased him, and to every seed his own body... There are also celestial bodies, and bodies terrestrial: but the glory of the celestial is one and the glory of the terrestrial is another... So also is the resurrection of the dead. It is sown in-corruption, it is raised in incorruption: It is sown in dishonor; it is raised in glory: It is sown in weakness; it is raised in power: It is sown a natural body, it is raised a spiritual body. There is a natural body, and there is a spiritual body... Behold I show you a mystery: We shall not all sleep, but we shall all be changed. In a moment, in the twinkling of an eye, at the last trumpet: for the trumpet shall sound, and the dead shall be raised incorruptible.*

In summary, we may describe the truths reported NDE cases as follows:

1. NDEs cannot be explained adequately on the basis of drugs, hallucinations, cultural conditioning, etc.

2. Religion, race and age are also unrelated to NDEs.

3. Ninety-five percent of NDEs are positive and literally transform the personality of the recipient. Many patients do not want to return to the physical body because it is so positive.

4. A Being of Light often conducts a panoramic life review of the patient during an NDE. Not only is every action observed, but the effects on others are noted. Telepathy is the mode of communication.

5. The patient sometimes gets information about the future. Some of these precognitions have been documented.

6. The overnight personality changes that occur, including greater zest for life, improved self-confidence, healthier eating habits and increased compassion, simply cannot be explained by hallucinations or any other conjecture proposed by the skeptics critical of this experience.

7. An NDE is one of the most powerful events a person can experience. It has redirected lives, created saints, inspired religions and shaped history.

8. NDEs are reported in 35 to 40 percent of people who have a brush with death.

Conscious Dying

To die, or cross into spirit, consciously, is to face clinical death without the loss of continuity of ones consciousness. This is the very essence of enlightenment and immortality. It is the only true path to liberation from the karmic cycle, or from the need to reincarnate over and over again until perfection is achieved.

At the moment of death our physical body clinically dies (including the ego), but our subconscious mind (soul) survives. If it can maintain direct contact with its perfect energy counterpart (superconscious mind or Higher Self) at this time, it will literally die consciously, the soul (subconscious mind) will be liberated, and spiritual growth will result.

However, if this contact is not maintained (unconscious death) then our soul will have missed a great opportunity for enlightenment and the most uncomfortable characteristics (the disorienting forces) of the karmic cycle will prevail.

Since the subconscious and superconscious mind (Higher Self) are actually energy, they cannot be destroyed. The first law of thermodynamics in physics clearly states that energy cannot be destroyed, merely altered in its form. For example, light can be transformed into electrical energy or heat, but the total amount of energy we end up with in this new form must equal that of the light at the start of the process.

The subconscious and Higher Self are, in reality, electromagnetic radiation. This harmless type of radiation is what comprises a television or radio signal.

To return to the concept of conscious dying, I refer you to Figure 3. Please note that the God energy overviews the entire process. The soul plane is where the soul goes between lifetimes to decide on its next life.

From the soul plane, most souls will experience the disorienting forces of the lower planes and goes through an unconscious rebirth into a physical body. All memories of its previous lives and its gestation on the soul plane will, for the most part, be lost. Throughout physical life consciousness is evident. Note the dotted lines that lead to altered states of consciousness (ASC). One form of ASC is an OBE (out-of-body experience).Note how the soul can leave and return from this experience.

The NDE (near-death experience) requires the body to literally die for a period from a few seconds to several minutes long. The NDE will result in either returning to the physical body or to actual death itself. From clinical death, you will note that the solid line returns to the disorienting forces of the lower planes. Then the Higher Self guides the subconscious back to the soul plane to choose its next lifetime. This is unconscious dying.

The Conscious Dying Process

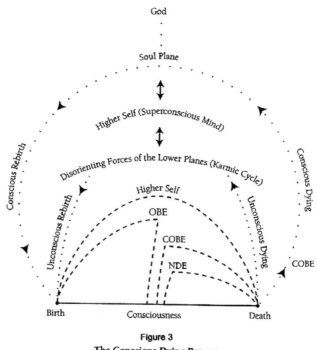

Figure 3
The Conscious Dying Process

The conscious dying process is illustrated by COBE (conscious out-of-body experience), during which our soul is carried through the death experience and avoids the karmic cycle on its return to the soul plane. When this liberated soul (subconscious mind) is reborn, it again avoids the karmic cycle interference and the conscious rebirth process is complete.

What is doing all of this traveling is the subconscious mind (soul). The Higher Self advises it and is also present throughout physical life. The Higher Self is especially pronounced on the soul plane. Note that the Higher Self is able to go to and from the soul plane, as indicated by the arrows going in both directions.

141

It is easy to see the many advantages that conscious dying has over the typical unconscious dying. Some of these advantages are:

- Shortening of our karmic cycle. This results in fewer remaining lifetimes.

- An increase in the quality of the remaining life.

- An instant recall of all past lives.

- Empowerment.

- Tremendous spiritual growth.

- An increase in psychic abilities.

- The elimination of the fear of death.

- Shorter bereavement (grief) experience for the loved ones left behind.

- An increase in the quality of the universe as a whole.

One of the main advantages in experiencing conscious dying is in discovering that the world beyond earth is merely another dimension of existence. It is a kind of "spiritual oasis" that nurtures and guides the soul as it continues to evolve higher in its return to the source from whence it came.

A Conscious Dying in a Hospital

Several years ago, I received an emergency call from a man concerning his wife. Norm had just admitted his wife Rose to Johns Hopkins Hospital for a severe pulmonary (lung) disorder. It seemed that Rose had use of only 20 percent of her lungs and the situation was medically critical.

Rose read my first book, *Past Lives-Future Lives* and wanted to experience a future life progression. She knew her time on the earth plane was about to expire. Several specialists examined her and were unanimous in their opinion of her condition. Rose did not have long to live.

Rose instructed her husband, Norm, to arrange for me to come to her hospital room to conduct hypnotherapy with her. Since Rose knew she was about to die, she wanted to be assured that she would live again in a new body at some future date.

Norm didn't share Rose's belief in reincarnation. He was aware of my reputation and respected me, but simply didn't think his wife or anyone else was capable of "coming back."

Since I have a hospital residency training as part of my post-graduate dental education, I did have hospital privileges with John Hopkins and arranged to meet with her. You can imagine the attitude of some of the more conventional physicians at this institution when I arrived.

My initial interview with Rose revealed several things. First, Rose was very depressed. She had had an unfulfilling life and was ill for most of it. Her relationship with Norm was far from ideal. Although Rose came from a wealthy family, this did not assure her happiness.

The second factor I observed was a diametrically opposite attitude between her physician and the nurses. Where the nurses were totally supportive of my work, Rose's lung specialist objected to my very presence. His objections were based solely on the fact that he did not believe in reincarnation and felt my presence would somehow embarrass him.

Fortunately, the hospital did not share his antagonism and allowed me to work with Rose. I was briefed by her specialist, who informed me that Rose had at most four weeks to live. Norm and Rose were told this and the prognosis did not help Rose's depressed state.

CHAPTER 7

I liked Rose from the moment I met her. She was truly motivated to work with me. As a lifelong believer in reincarnation (this is not necessary for conscious dying to be effective), Rose was well read and an excellent hypnotic patient.

Rose did ask me if I would allow several of her nurses to witness her therapy. Naturally, I had no objection to this. My sessions were done with Norm and between three and six nurses present.

I did take a brief history from Rose and discovered that she did not lead a happy life. As a woman in her sixties with no children and only Norm at her side, she appeared almost numb. She did not love Norm and never had. All through her life Rose was depressed and victimized by a long string of psychosomatic illnesses. She had respiratory (breathing) problems through most of her life. Looking at her lack of emotional expression, I could see why she was ready to die.

Norm informed me of Rose's unhappy life and felt somewhat guilty about his role in it. He really tried to make her happy, but he had many problems of his own.

The nurses were helpful to me in providing additional background to Rose's state of mind since she was admitted, in addition to the medications she was taking. Rose was continually monitored by various machines, so it was not easy to move around in her room.

My initial session with her ended with a lengthy hypnotic trance and a superconscious mind scan of several of her past lives. I then initiated a cleansing to train her to raise the frequency vibrational rate of her subconscious (soul). Finally a future life progression was conducted.

During Rose's future life, in the middle of the twenty-first century she saw herself as a happy young woman involved with charitable institutions. She helped many people far less fortunate than herself. In addition, she had a husband and two children and was very happy.

Up to this time Rose expressed no emotions. She was merely depressed and could hardly speak. Now she cried with joy

144

and began to act in an animated fashion. This welcome change shocked Norm and the nurses, who were not accustomed to seeing Rose act this way.

At the end of this long session I told Rose and Norm that I would return the following day and the rest of the week would be spent training Rose in the art of conscious dying.

They readily agreed and Rose acted like a child with a new toy. I gave her some self-hypnosis tapes to play to assist her orientation of the techniques. Each day I spent at Johns Hopkins was more rewarding than the day before. Rose responded quite well and Norm appeared to change his attitude to what I was doing.

The hospital spread the word quickly about my work with Rose. Each day I saw different nurses and interns who wanted to witness the therapy for themselves. Rose now could laugh and cry. She still had problems speaking and breathing, but this was most definitely a different person.

Although the staff asked a lot of questions about the theoretical foundation for what I was doing, my time had to be spent clinically attending to Rose. They were very considerate and patiently waited until I took a break in the clinical procedures before questioning me.

I felt as though I was conducting a workshop, spending every coffee break and lunch break discussing the details and theoretical basis of karma, reincarnation, quantum physics, and conscious dying.

As the end of each week and the completion of my therapy with Rose approached, Norm appeared to change his lifelong opinion about reincarnation. He could not believe the complete change in Rose's demeanor. For the first time since he had known her, Rose appeared to be at peace. The expression "at peace" was repeated to me by the nurses and Rose herself several times. This is one of the many benefits of conscious dying. The cleansing experienced by the patient without exception results in a state of mind of peace and tranquility.

Just before I left the hospital for the last time, I spoke to Rose about all that we had accomplished. This was not just a summary of our treatment or a wrap-up session. I explained that she very soon would have the opportunity to apply these techniques. She understood me and asked some very pertinent questions.

The last words Rose said to me were "God bless you and your work." Two weeks later Norm called to let me know that Rose died. He was with her up to the. very end. Just before she died she was smiling and said to him, "The doctor was right, I am ready."

A Documented Case of Conscious Dying

When I first began my work with past life regression in 1974, critics would always say that you cannot prove reincarnation. I agree, but you can present suggestive evidence establishing the hypothesis that the soul lives on in other physical bodies. The only way to do that is to check out and corroborate the data given by the patient during a regression. This has been done many thousands of times by various researchers.

However, my second book, *The Search for Grace*, describes a case of reincarnation that was fully validated by an independent researcher hired by CBS television. This case, based on a regression in 1988, was dramatized in the television movie *Search for Grace* starring Lisa Hartman and Ken Wahl, which first aired on May 17, 1994. Most significant about the documentation was that two facts the patient told me in trance did not check out with newspaper records of the time (1929). In regression she told me that she was thirty-two years old when she died and that her sons name was Cliff. Newspaper reports stated that Grace Doze was thirty years old and referred to her son as Chester, Jr.

A subsequent search for Grace Dozes birth certificate revealed that my patient was correct and the Buffalo newspaper reporters had made minor errors. Since New York is a closed state and political permission (along with a written request filed with the

146

state) is required to obtain these records, it would have been impossible for my patient to have known the true facts prior to 1992 when the research was done. (I had regressed the patient [Ivy] in 1988.) This fact was verified when a representative from the department of public records was interviewed on a local radio station in Buffalo the day the television movie aired. I was also interviewed on the same show.

The reason I discuss this case here is to show the potential problems involved with documentation. It is difficult enough to corroborate a past life. How can one possibly document a case of conscious dying?

Since the patient leaves the earth plane when they consciously die, all communication with me is terminated. The following case, I believe, illustrates not only the benefits of conscious dying, but also gives highly suggestive evidence of a documented case of this experience.

In 1979 a sixty-four-year-old woman came to my office. Edna was dying of cancer and had only a few months to live. When I interviewed her I observed a depressed and lonely woman more afraid of living than of dying.

Edna was a widow and had one son who had died as a teenager many years before in a car accident. She had few friends and felt abandoned by her family. Although she was depressed she was not suicidal. She did not look forward to the next day but was not afraid to die.

Edna long ago had abandoned her belief in God. Her life was so stressful and characterized by so many losses that she believed in nothing. The idea of reincarnation was attractive to her philosophically, but she just was not sure what happened after she died.

The only joy she had in life was playing the piano. Since she was a child she had played classical music on this instrument, but now, due to arthritis and her generally weakened medical condition, this became impossible. She could no longer play the piano.

CHAPTER 7

Edna's life was one tragedy and loss after another. She was always indecisive, even as a child. Her family nicknamed her "Iffy" to reflect this personality trait of saying, "If only I had done this..."

When I worked with her, several past-life regressions were conducted at her request. She reported several traumatic and unhappy previous lifetimes. Her indecisiveness was exhibited in most of these lives. Interestingly enough, one somewhat positive lifetime was characterized by her playing the piano as a school teacher in the 1800s.

These regressions helped Edna deal with the idea of the immortality of her soul. She was not interested in perceiving a future lifetime, but several conscious dying sessions were conducted. During these cleansings she referred to her spirit guide as Shamani.

Edna appeared much less depressed when I completed her training. She appeared ready to accept and deal with her pending transition and to apply her conscious dying techniques. Her neighbor always brought Edna to my office and further reinforced my observations.

I will always remember our last conversation. Just before leaving my office for the last time she took my hand and said, "we will meet again." Although that is not unusual to hear from a patient, it is the first' time someone with just a few months to live said that to me. Two months later Edna's neighbor informed me that Edna died. The death was reportedly a peaceful one as Edna died with a smile on her face.

In 1988 a couple from the Midwest called my office and made an appointment for their seven-year-old daughter, Paula. This couple was very conventional and had no belief in reincarnation.

Paula's mother saw me conduct a past life regression on the *Phil Donahue Show* and expressed concern about Paula's mental state. She felt I was the perfect therapist for her daughter.

When they arrived at my office, I obtained a detailed history of Paula's problem. Ever since she began speaking, Paula made several references to her lost family. She talked about her son and husband and how difficult it was to be an old lady living alone. Paula also showed natural talent and interest in playing the piano. She especially liked playing classical music. This hobby pleased her parents, but it was her earlier behavior that concerned them.

Paula's parents felt that she was "possessed" by some evil spirit and requested that I exorcise this demon out of her. I work with many children in my practice. Paula's attitude and mannerisms were those of a bright, creative, communicative, and happy child. Her parents' concerns were well meaning but my interpretation of Paula's behavior was that she was expressing the mannerisms of her last life.

Paula was in second grade and a model student. She had playmates, but preferred the company of adults, especially her grandparents.

Paula asked if I would mind calling her by her nickname. I said, "of course not," and asked her what that name was. I was literally shocked when she said "Iffy." Her parents confirmed that Paula liked to be called Iffy, but they just could not adopt it as her nickname.

Both parents were present when I regressed Paula to her last life. She related to me the story of Edna. Several facts were easily confirmed by my records, and when I conducted this past life regression I had Edna's chart on my desk for reference.

During a superconscious mind tap Paula again shocked me. She spoke of the soul plane and of her guide. She then said, "Shamani says hi." This was the name Edna used to describe her Higher Self.

Paula was born in 1981, just two years after Edna died. Paula could barely read and never read books on reincarnation. Her parents did not believe in past lives, and had absolutely no incentive to have their daughter lie to me. In addition, they could not possibly have known Edna, who had few friends and lived over 1,500 miles away.

CHAPTER 7

There is no logical or conventional explanation for this case. Apparently Edna had to reincarnate but she chose a life in which she is happy and well adjusted. Edna can again play the piano. Since she was consciously reborn she has memories of her past lives.

Welcome back, Edna. Yes, we did meet again and thank you from the depths of my soul for your documented case of conscious dying and conscious rebirth.

Instructions for Using the Conscious Dying Script/Tape

To prepare for this experience, I recommend:

1. Do this at a time that you will not be disturbed. Make sure that no deadline or time limit is set.

2. Lie down or place yourself in whatever position you find most conducive to relaxation. Loosen any clothing that feels tight or distracting in any way. Feel free to take off your shoes and be sure to remove any jewelry. Darken the room, but avoid a pitch-black environment.

3. Since in the COBE state you are subjected to every thought that crosses your mind, close your mind to any thoughts or focus on a single thought as best you can.

4. To facilitate leaving the physical body, think of getting lighter and of floating upward. Focus on how nice it would be to do this.

5. Keep all concentration on a single goal, one at a time. Refrain from distracting thoughts. Mentally tell yourself that you can see and communicate with your Higher Self.

6. For traveling while out of the body you must go to a person and not a place. Think not only of the persons name but of

the character and personality of this individual. Do not try to visualize a physical person. Focus instead on the inner person.

7. Merely thinking of your physical body will initiate the return process. Mentally, then physically, move a finger or toe, or take a deep breath, and your soul will immediately return to the physical body. This technique is perfectly safe.

8. Open up your eyes and sit up after this re-entry. You will be able to do anything else that you have planned for the day or evening.

Here is the script of the conscious out-of-body experience:

> **Now listen very carefully. I want you to imagine a bright white light coming down from above and entering the top of your head. Filling your entire body. See it, feel it and it becomes reality. Now imagine an aura of pure white light emanating from your heart region. Again surrounding your entire body. Protecting you. See it, feel it, and it becomes reality. Now only your Masters and Guides Higher Self and highly evolved loving entities who mean well will be able to influence you during this or any other hypnotic session. You are totally protected by this aura of pure white light.**
>
> **Now focus in on how comfortable and relaxed you are, free of distractions, free from physical and emotional obstacles that prevent you from safely leaving and returning to the physical body. You will perceive and remember all that you encounter during this experience. You will recall in detail when you are physically awake only these matters that will be beneficial**

to your physical and mental being and experience. Now begin to sense the vibrations around you, and in your own mind begin to shape and pull them into a ring around your head. Do this for a few moments now.

PLAY NEW AGE MUSIC FOR 2 MINUTES.[*]

Now as you begin to attract these vibrations into your inner awareness, they begin to seep throughout your body making it rigid and immobile. You are always in complete control of this experience. Do this now as you perceive yourself rigid and immobile with these vibrations moving along and throughout your entire body.

PLAY NEW AGE MUSIC FOR 2 MINUTES.

You have done very well. Pulse these vibrations. Perceive yourself feeling the pulse of these vibrations throughout your entire awareness. In your own mind's eye, reach out one of your arms and grasp some object that you know is out of normal reach. Feel the object and let your astral hand pass through it. Your mind is using your astral arm, not your physical arm, to feel the object. As you do this you are becoming lighter and lighter and your astral body is beginning to rise up from your physical body. Do this now.

---

[*]   Dr. Goldberg's website has special New Age music for these exercises.

PLAY NEW AGE MUSIC FOR 2 MINUTES.

You've done very well. Now using other parts of your astral body (your head, feet, chest and back) repeat this exercise and continue to feel lighter and lighter as your astral body begins to rise up from your physical body. Do this now.

PLAY NEW AGE MUSIC FOR 2 MINUTES.

Now think of yourself as becoming lighter and lighter throughout your body. Perceive yourself floating up as your entire astral body lifts up and floats away from your physical body. Concentrate on blackness and remove all fears during this process. Imagine a helium-filled balloon rising and pulling your astral body with it up and away from your physical body. Do this now.

PLAY NEW AGE MUSIC FOR 2 MINUTES.

See how easy it is to leave the body while remaining in complete contact with your Higher Self. This is the process of conscious dying. it is that simple. Now ask your Higher Self for any instruction that will assist your spiritual growth. Remember, your Higher Self is all knowledgeable and has access to your Akashic records.

Now slowly and carefully state your desire for information or an experience and let your Higher Self work for you. Let it help you raise your soul's energy.

PLAY NEW AGE MUSIC FOR 3 MINUTES.

You have done very well. Now I want you to further open up the channels of communication by removing any obstacles and allowing yourself to receive information and experiences that will directly apply to and help better your present lifetime. Allow yourself to receive more advanced and more specific information from your Higher Self and Masters and Guides to raise your frequency and improve your karmic subcycle.

Maintain the communication and connection with your Higher Self. You are one with your Higher Self. This connection will always exist, even when the physical body dies. Allow your Higher Self to instruct you. Do this now.

PLAY NEW AGE MUSIC FOR 3 MINUTES.

Alright now. Sleep now and rest. You did very, very well. Listen very carefully. I'm going to count forward now from 1 to 5. When I reach the count of 5 you will be back in your physical body. You will be able to remember everything you experienced and re-experienced, you'll feel very relaxed, refreshed, you'll be able to do whatever you have planned for the rest of the day or evening.

154

You'll feel very positive about what you've just experienced and very motivated about your confidence and ability to play this tape again to experience conscious dying. Alright now. 1 very, very deep, 2 you're getting a little bit lighter, 3 you're getting much, much lighter, 4 very, very light, 5 awaken. Wide awake and refreshed.

You can order my Conscious Dying Training Program from my website for a complete set of CDs to do these techniques.

---

[1]   Raymond A. Moody, Jr., *Life After Life*, Bantam Books, New York, 1975.

[2]   Kenneth Ring, *Life At Death*. Coward, McCann & Geoghegan, New York, 1980, p. 41-42.

[3]   Robert Crookall, *The Study and Practice of Astral Projection*, Aquarian Press, London, 1961.

[4]   Karlis Osis and Erlendur Haroldsson, *At the Hour of Death*, Avon, New York, 1977, p. 168.

[5]   Raymond A. Moody, Jr., *Life After Life*, Bantam Books, New York, 1975.

[6]   Ibid.

[7]   Michael B. Sabom, *Recollections of Death: A Medical Investigation*, Harper & Row, New York, 1982, p. 41.

[8]   Ibid. p. 43.

[9]   Raymond A. Moody, Jr., *The Light Beyond*, Bantam Books, New York, 1988, p. 50.

[10]   Michael B. Sabom, p. 50-51.

[11]   Raymond A. Moody, Jr., *The Light Beyond*, Bantam Books, New York, 1988, p. 87.

[12]   Michael B. Sabom, op. cit.

[13]   Raymond A. Moody, Jr., *Life After Life*.

[14]   Ibid.

[15]   Kenneth Ring, *Life At Death*.

[16]   Ibid.

CHAPTER 8

THE TRUTH ABOUT TIME

One advantage of exploring the fifth dimension is that all time is simultaneous, so we can view past and future events (including parallel universes). Throughout history, the concept of time has perplexed man. Even today, there are conflicting ideas about the fourth dimension. Linear time versus space time continues to be debated among people all over our planet. The twentieth century philosopher, Henri Bergson, stated that understanding the nature of time is the key to the main problems of philosophy. It is also an important component of the ultimate truth.

William James averred in his book, *The Principles of Psychology*, that the "prototype of all conceived times is the specious present, the short duration of which we are immediately and incessantly sensible." Thus, James' approach is that all other temporal concepts can be defined in terms. of the relation "earlier than" and that this relation is sense given or can be ostensibly defined so that even if a person does not use the term "specious present," he is obliged to say that some earlier events are still, in some sense, present to us when we are sensing a later event.[1]

CHAPTER 8

It was E.R. Clay, who coined the term, specious present, to refer to the durationless instant between past and future. It may be easier to imagine time as a line of which the specious present is a segment whose later boundary is the real present and hence concluded that the specious present and its contents are really past.

James said that the specious present has "a vaguely vanishing backward and forward fringe," and that it is "a saddle-back from which we look in two directions in time."[2] We are, therefore, continuously directly perceiving or intuiting a past duration and its contents.

When one assumes time to be the fourth dimension, then the physical world is view as changeless. It is our states of consciousness that change as we become successively aware of adjacent cross-sections of the four-dimensional world. But this makes sense only if we, the observers, are not in space time (and one would still have to acknowledge a [real] time dimension other than the one which has been spatialized, in which our states of consciousness are successive).

Apart from its later boundary the specious present is really past, and he is thereby disposed to say (1) that the contents of the specious present consist of images or "representations" of what has just been sensed and (2) that what these images represent is known only by memory. Here we have a second way of describing the relevant experiences.

St. Augustine in *Confessions*[3] stated that the present has no duration. He assumed that everything which is past, or future, does not now exist. When a person perceives or measures time, what he is attending to is "something which remains fixed in his memory" and therefore that time is not "something objective." He ended by, in effect, defining "past" in terms of human memories and "future" in terms of human expectations. These conclusions suited Augustine, for his purpose in discussing time was to show that it is meaningless to ask what God was doing before he made heaven and earth.

Space-time and quantum physics would disagree with these conclusions, and we will deal with the new physics in the next chapter. Few philosophers, today, would accept the notion that time (conceived of as an infinite continuum) is an intuited datum.

Time, according to most philosophers, is a concept that we devise from temporal relations, which are sense given. They accept the idea that these temporal relations occur within the present and might better be called "the conscious present." Clay and James called this duration "the specious [that is, pseudo] present," because they assumed that only its later boundary should be called "the real present."[4]

We must not think in terms of time moving along a line. Events cannot actually move or change. Things change, while events merely happen. It can be said that time is a nonspatial order in which things change. Events, on the other hand, are changes in three dimensional things. The spatialized concept of time being thought of as an intellectual construct incorrectly represents real time, which belongs only to inner consciousness. Thus, our consciousness of time's flow is our consciousness of things changing.

One of the greatest shocks to man's conception of time and his place in the universe occurred in the middle of the nineteenth century, with Darwin's theory of evolution. Despite its obvious effect on the biological and geological sciences, it raised certain questions concerning the soul that it was simply incapable of answering. It could not satisfactorily explain what was the ultimate meaning of man's place in the universe - the ultimate truth?

Darwinian *Origin of Species*[5] could only speculate on the meaning of life from a strictly temporal vantage point. More specifically, what was the mode of thoughts of our primitive ancestors? Theories of origins - the origin of society, of religion, of mythology and many more - flourished; but almost without exceptions they attributed modern attitudes to the past. It was assumed that the thought processes of primitive man must be accessible to the investigator, and this assumption gave rise to considerable speculation concerning the nature of primitive mentality, but in the absence of all but the most ambiguous evidence, such theories were never far removed from sheer guesswork.

Mircea Eliade, a Romanian religious historian, in his book, *Cosmos and History: The Myth of the Eternal Return*, attempts to account for the essential differences between the mind of primitive man and that of the mind of modern man in the Judaeo-Christian tradition. Eliade suggests that primitive man feared the passage of time and dealt with this fear by a repeated return to a mythical past (the Eternal Return); Judaeo-Christian man, on the other hand, recognizes God at work within history, and can thus accept his historical existence and his own place in history without fear. In Eliade's own words:

> *The chief difference between the man of the archaic and traditional societies and the man of the modern societies with their strong imprint of Judaeo-Christianity lies in the fact that the former feels himself indissolubly connected with the Cosmos and the cosmic rhythms, whereas the latter insists that he is connected only with History.[6]*

Time has always been important to primitive man. The recurrence of day and night, the phases of the moon, the reproductive cycles of man and other animals, and the progression of the seasons are well represented in primitive religions. Just as creation itself is believed to have been a conquest of chaos, so each new fertile season and each new beginning is seen as a repetition of the same creative act.

Eliade states primitive man believed that "everything begins over again at its commencement every instant. The past is but a prefiguration of the future. No event is irreversible and no transformation is final." The beginning of a new year was looked upon as a repetition of what has already been, not something new. What has been before is the creative action of the universe.

The *Enuma elish* of ancient Mesopotamia (Iraq) at the New Year (Akitu), is a recitation of the epic of creation. First chaos is temporarily re-established, as the king is deprived of his symbols of office; but then the creation of the world is re-enacted: the fates are cast for the subsequent twelve months, and finally the fertility of the land, man and beast is symbolically ensured by an act of hierogamy - ritual intercourse between the king and a priestess.

This view of life solves the problem of pain and suffering. These societies never felt these things just happened, but were caused by something. The Hindu doctrine of karma provides one possible explanation: suffering is brought about by moral and ritual lapses in a previous cycle of existence. Elsewhere, the suffering of a god or goddess may be postulated, and this, too, provides a consolation, since the sufferer knows that his unhappiness is shared. Thus, the death of the deity of agriculture at the onset of winter, or the dry season, is representative of this suffering. When spring comes, renewal is evidenced by the rebirth of this god.

This knowledge that the cosmos "dies" periodically and is renewed, was comforting to primitive man. It allowed him to deal with his difficult life. The belief in reincarnation and a better future life was his only salvation.

The mystery religions offered precisely this - assimilation by initiation to gods and goddesses (Isis, Osiris, Demeter, Persephone, Orpheus and many more), who themselves shared in the earth's universal pattern of death and resurrection. The mysteries provided a form of security in the fact of the trials and tribulations of mortal life. They abolished the "terror or history" by offering an eternal return. This is not to say that reincarnation isn't real. It may, in fact, be the main component of the Ultimate Truth.

Christianity and Judaism mostly promulgated the concept of linear time. For centuries, this view was superimposed on the cyclical view of the common man, and was, thus, not generally accepted. In the eighteenth and nineteenth centuries, Westerner's truth taught man to look to the future, not the past, for fulfillment. Ideas of progress replaced the cyclical theories of time. Every event was regarded as unique, irreversible and a new manifestation of the will of God, especially in Christian theology.

Man began to shift his obsession from writing history to the spinning of dreams of a utopian future. Note how utopian dreams and the prediction of catastrophe constitute the main themes of science fiction.

Modern man has not lost his attraction to the timeless world of universal myth. Today, we create our truths in the form of myths out of pop singers, athletes and film stars. We no longer use the ancient philosophy of a world shaped by gods. The disappointing effect of our current approach is that our celebrities may give us a fleeting moment of distraction to the stresses of the world, but they cannot give us the immortality that we so desire.

A different view of primitive man was presented by Professor S.G.F. Brandon, in his book, *History, Time and Deity.*[7] He states that the Egyptian and Mesopotamian civilizations were not afraid of history. They perpetuated the memory of their achievements, in dynastic lists, commemorative inscriptions (in the most durable of materials), portraits and autobiographical funerary texts, recording not only names but deeds. As Brandon writes, "Such records of the past clearly attest a belief in the unique and definitive nature of the events thus commemorated as well as the conviction that the memory of them was worth preserving."

We, in the West, base our current "rational" thinking on the models proposed in ancient Greece. The Greek philosopher, Democritus, talked about the atom. Pythagorus, Aristotle, Archimedes and others led the way to the development of Western science today.

The Greeks studied the concept of time by first dealing with the notion of the continuity of motion.

This concept of the continuity of motion was represented by two quite different approaches. Zeno popularized the idea of the discontinuity of motion by illustrating that there is a difference between what we see occurring, and what we mean by it. He demonstrated that the motion of an object actually consisted of consecutive still frames, as in a motion picture film.

Aristotle countered this truth by demonstrating that motion (and, thus, time) occurred as a continuous whole. He stated that motion was a continuous stream of inseparable still events. This theory won out and paralyzed Zeno's truth of discontinuity, for 2,500 years. Aristotle's concept of continuous functions is the basis of modern calculus. It was not until the quantum physicists discovered the discontinuous motion of atomic particles, that Zeno's truth was proven correct.

Zeno was the first quantum physicist and he based his truth on three paradoxes. The question he pondered was, "How can we understand movement, if an object is to occupy a given place at a given time?" An object must occupy a given place at a given time, for it cannot occupy more than its given place at anyone time or it would have to be in two or more places at the same time. We must assume a given object must occupy a given place at a given time and certainly no more. Zeno's first paradox stated that motion cannot exist because in order for a runner, for example, to reach the endpoint of his race, he must first reach the point halfway between the endpoint and the starting point. The runner must go at least halfway to the goal line before he can cross it. But the paradox is that before he can reach the halfway point, he must reach the point midway between the halfway point and the starting line. This statement can be applied to any distance in this race. Before the runner can reach the quarterway point, he must reach the one-eighthway point, and before that, the one-sixteenthway point, etc. There are an infinite number of these halfway points, and each of them marks off a finite distance the runner must reach before he can go on to the next point. Therefore, there is no first distance he can run to. Thus, motion and, subsequently, time does not exist.

Zeno's second paradox states that a runner (1) can never overtake a runner (2) ahead of him. To do so, runner (1) must first reach the point just departed by runner (2). Since there are an infinite number of such points, runner (2) will always have left any point before runner (1) arrives there.

The third paradox proposed by Zeno demonstrates that an arrow cannot fly. We must assume that an object is continually moving or continually at rest. At any instant, the arrow is occupying a certain place. If it is occupying a place, it must be at rest there. The arrow must be at rest at the instant we picture, and since the instant we have chosen is any instant; the arrow cannot be moving at any instant. Thus the arrow is always at rest and cannot fly.

Zeno deduced that neither motion nor time actually exist. They only appear to exist. Filmmakers, today, use Zeno's conclusions to create animated movies. They shoot each frame as a still photograph and combine several thousand of these in the final product. They would agree that an object in a film scene must be at rest in each frame it occupies.

In the next chapter, we will more thoroughly discuss the new physics and its interpretation of time and the universe in general.

---

[1]   William James, *The Principles of Psychology*, Henry Holt, New York, 1890.
[2]   Ibid.
[3]   St. Augustine, *Confessions*, translated by Vernon J. Bourke, Fathers of the Church, Inc., New York, 1953.
[4]   Mircea Eliade, *Cosmos and History: The Myth of the Eternal Return*, Harper and Row Torchbooks, New York, 1959.
[5]   Charles Darwin, *Origin of Species*, Prometheus Books, Buffalo, N.Y., 1991.
[6]   Mircea Eliade, op. cit.
[7]   S. F. Brandon, *History, Time and Deity*, Barnes and Noble, New York, 1965.

CHAPTER 9

THE TRUTH FROM QUANTUM PHYSICS

We will discuss the scientific basis for parallel universes. The new physics or quantum physics (technically, quantum mechanics), states and establishes the principle of parallel universes. We will devote most of our discussion to the truths about other universes existing along with ours, according to the truths of the new physics.

The Principle Of Uncertainty

Quantum physics tells us that we can define only what we can measure. The concepts of position and motion are dubious at best, since we cannot measure both the momentum and the position of any object with exact precision. The more we know of the position of an electron, for example, the less we know of its future path or momentum. The quantum physicist, Werner Heisenberg, solved this dilemma by stating that the path of any object comes into existence only when we observe it. This came to be known as Heisenberg's Principle of Indeterminism (often referred to as the Principle of Uncertainty). Heisenberg was awarded the Nobel prize in physics for his affirmation that Zeno (see chapter 8) was correct, "An object cannot occupy a given place and be moving at the same time."[1]

Before we consider the specifics of these other universes, some background concerning time travel needs to be presented. Einstein stated that it would be impossible to travel faster than the speed of light, since it would require an infinite amount of energy to accelerate a body to that speed. Quantum physicists today disagree and postulate the existence of just such particles and calls them tachyons. A tachyon already in existence is not refuted by relativity.

Since these hypothetical particles travel faster than light, they would observe events in a reverse order. In other words, any object or a consciousness traveling faster than the speed of light would not be confined by space and time. It could travel anywhere and at any moment in our past or future in an instant. Tachyons do not experience real time. They are, thus, able to move backward and forward in their imaginary time dimension as easily as you go back and forth from your living room, but we would experience tachyons in real time.

Quantum physicists mathematically demonstrate that an event must be observed to be a component of reality. Our entire universe is a product of our mind. One only needs to change one's mind to alter this reality. The world appears as a by-product of this form of mental gymnastics. Failing to achieve dramatic results, such as traveling back or forward in time, are due to a mere lack of imagination. The new physics tells us that it is our observations that actually determine and shape events in our life. We are not mere observers, nor can we separate ourselves from the events we see.

In 1905, Einstein completely revised the classical notions of time with his special theory of relativity. For one thing, he formally connected space and time into one entity, space-time. Henceforth, all discussions about space involved discussions about time, and vice-versa. Einstein also abolished the concept of a universal, linear flow of time, since different observers may perceive different sequences for events when they move with different velocities relative to the observed events. If the observer happened to be moving towards the location of the event on his right, away from the event on his left, he would see the "right" event occurring before the "left" one. And, conversely, if he happened to be moving towards the "left" event, away from the "right" one, he would observe the "left" event occurring earlier than the "right."

Matter was now thought of as a by product of energy and a knot in the fabric of space-time. Matter bent space and curved time. This made it possible to envision just how the universe could have begun. Not only was the universe created from light energy, but light spends no time in the universe it created. It always travels at 186,000 miles per second and can't really exist in one place for an instant. This zero .time quality makes photons (light particles or waves) exist on a borderline between solid, tangible and the ethereal, potential. Photons are all of these simultaneously. As we shall see, these photons are the result of matter and anti-matter colliding.

Einstein's theory of relativity predicted the existence of alternate universes. A graduate student at Princeton University, also the home of Einstein, received a Ph.D. in quantum mechanics in 1957, while delineating the specifics of the parallel universe concept. This student was named Hugh Everett III. Everett showed that the entire universe is connected through these parallel universes.

The truths about parallel universes were further expanded in 1969 at Brown University, when physicists Leon N. Cooper and Deborah Van Veckten demonstrated that whenever a measurement of a physical system occurs, the system appears to "jump" into one of many possible physical states. The system cannot exist in any of these states before the measurement is made. Their conclusion proved that whenever a measurement takes please, the universe splits into as many universes as there are possibilities.

CHAPTER 9

Black Holes

General relativity theory under the maximum stress of matter's distortion of space and time predicts that existence of a black hole, the most distorting region of space-time anywhere, anytime. And spinning black holes contain bridges connecting our universe to parallel universes. Einstein's curved space-time resulted in what mathematicians call singularities. These are actually bridges between gravity and parallel universes. Tremendous distortions, possibly tears in the fabric of space-time, occur in these regions. These singularities exist in the center of a black hole and all physical quantities take on infinite values at these locations. At the center of this black hole, light stops moving. Gateways to parallel universes exist by these distortions. Einstein and Rosen discovered these and we refer to this connection between parallel worlds as the Einstein-Rosen bridge.

Space and time exhibit a reversal, as one passes from one universe to another through a black hole. As a space traveler approached a future singularity, we would observe him moving backward in time. The singularity would still be in the future for him, but not for us. In fact, if we could watch all this happen we would see two travelers, one approaching the black hole from the outside, and one escaping the black hole from the inside. From our vantage point, this would occur at the same time.

Let us take a detailed look at this singularity. As we approach the outermost zone, the static limit, any light we emit is pulled in the direction of the rotation of this black hole. As we move inside the static limit, we find ourselves in what is called the ergosphere. It is an energetic zone where light is both swept around and gravitationally pulled toward the hole's center. Next we cross the outer event horizon. In the region bounded by this sphere and another sphere called the inner event horizon, space and time have turned topsy-turvy. As soon as we cross the inner event horizon, space and time reverse again and the world becomes normal. However, we will exit this back hole through a white hole and enter a parallel universe, which may be the past or the future of the universe we formerly called home.

If we remain outside of the static limit and event horizons, every thing seems normal. It is only when we cross over through both inner and outer event horizons, we would find things had reversed. Instead of being pulled back into the hole, we would be compelled to move onward and outward, passing through the outer event horizon (once we have crossed the inner one) into another universe through a white hole.

The white hole forces everything out, while the black hole sucks everything (including light) into it. From the perspective of the white hole side, we would experience the past being pulled beyond us into the white hole. This would give the appearance of a universe running backward in time. The inhabitants of this new and parallel universe would find nothing unusual about their environment, even though their time flows in the opposite direction to the universe we previously knew.

The unique feature of all black holes is the one-wayness of the event horizons surrounding them. Once you cross the boundary, space and time reverse, trapping you and making you move onward in space and onward in time. You are now caught in the timestream and cannot turn around. Whenever a black 'hole is created, a white must form too.

Antimatter

Einstein's famous equation, E MC², equates energy and matter. This led to speculation that matter may be trapped light energy. In quantum physics. a process known as electron-positron annihilation, and its counterpart, electron-positron creation, led to an important truth about parallel universes. When an electron collides with its parallel universe counterpart (antimatter) , known as a positron, both disappear. The result of this annihilation is two particles of light called photons. Electrons can do this because it is suspected that they may travel faster than the speed of light. If the light energy is high enough, the photons can be turned back into matter and antimatter again.

The properties of a positron are almost identical to that of an electron. The only difference is that everything is reversed. The electrical charge of the electron is negative, while the positron has a positive charge. The positron's spin direction is opposite to the electron's. It is theorized, according to one of the truths of quantum physics, that the electron is a positron moving backward in time and vice versa. This would enable it to be in two places simultaneously. The opposite particle (electron or positron) would now appear as a particle with opposite properties we observe for its partner.

Consciousness

In order for there to be consciousness, there must be choice. The new physics clearly demonstrates that we choose between alternatives and this helps create and shape our reality, including parallel universes. Since there must be mind to make these choices, there must be consciousness. One truth that quantum physics relates to us is that mind exists as fleeting energy in parallel universes. The overlapping of these fleeting flashes of energy makes up the universe we perceive. These patterns create both mind and matter. It is the mind (consciousness) of human beings that perceives reality and selects that reality from various other universes. Consciousness is thought of as being able to travel faster than light, thus, it may go back or forward in time instantaneously.

Superspace

Parallel universe truths[2] require an object in space to exist in all of the spaces in these universes at the same time. It occupies only a single point, when we observe this object. Prior to this observation, the objects in each space pass through each other's spaces like ghosts in the night. These objects, I must point out, are quite solid in their own separate space.

The term superspace is used to describe this concept. There is always room for another universe, another whole space, in superspace. In it, objects take on individual, but separate realities. And all of those realities move like ripples in the wind of probability. Thus, superspace is an imaginary mathematical construct used to depict circumstances in which there are more than three dimensions. Superspace contains points just as ordinary space does. But each point in superspace marks the locations of every object in a whole universe. That is, each point in superspace is a scale model of a whole and distinct universe.

Holograms

A hologram may be described as a photographic record of light waves reflected by an object. A laser light illuminates this object. The combination of the direct light from the source (laser) and the reflected light from the object, results in an interference pattern on the photographic plate. A three-dimensional image of the object can then be produced by illuminating the interference pattern with the original laser light.

This interference pattern contains all of the visual information from the object. Thus, the entire object is represented in each region of the photographic plate. The three-dimensional object can be made to appear, if only a small section of the plate is illuminated. Because the light from all points on the object is enfolded into each area of the photographic plate, each section in holography is related to the entire structure

The quantum physicist, David Bohn, states that quantum particles function as holograms. His truth says that when a particle taps into the information field, its movement reflects the state of the whole. Thus, the particle cannot be separated from its environment and cannot be treated as an independent entity; it is an aspect of the entire system.

In other words, any event occurring anywhere is immediately available everywhere as information. Each portion of space contains information about all portions of space. The reason the classical world appears to us as separate and distinct objects is because the quantum potential at the macro level is negligible. Bohm's truth is that all information is enfolded within each region ,and is, therefore, available to all particles, and all quantum fields of all particles have an input in every area.

Communication With the Past and Future

The existence of parallel universes makes possible the communication with the past and future through quantum wave probability, since this wave can travel back and forward in time. One question this truth brings to mind is what happens if I go back in time and alter the past? You may change the course of history in one parallel universe, but the others would not be affected by this alteration.

The new physics tells us that quantum wave probabilities imply the existence of both the past and future simultaneously with our own time. A future "me" is sending back-through-time quantum waves, which will clash with the waves being generated here and now.

If these wave resonances match, the future and present event become meaningful to me and a real future is created along with memory sequences. If there is no resonance, then, there will be no probability of a connection between the present and future. It will not occur in my awareness. This truth tells us that the greater the probability, the more meaningful the transaction, and the greater the chance of it occurring.

The closer in "time" the sources of these waves are, the more likely that the two countertime quantum wave streams will "marry" and produce a strong probability - one that has a good chance of becoming real. One explanation for visionaries is the ability to marry quantum wave streams originating from far time-distant sources. People who lack the ability to do this for the shortest time-distances would be unable to cope with life.

A timeless state would result if we were able to marry corresponding times every moment of our time-bound existences.

This is possible, since the past, present, and future exist side-by-side as simultaneous time. This timeless state is considered to be our base state of reality (the truth) by many forms of spiritual practices. The only reason we don't do this is because of our failure to discriminate between the many past and future sending stations attempting to communicate with us. We, thus, live time-bound lives, disconnected from the past and the future.

People who are capable of lucid dreaming, those we label as schizophrenic, and visionaries, may be able to receive these signals from the future clearer than the rest of-us. UFO sightings, other paranormal phenomena, along with insights and psychotic behavior, may just be due to an individual lost in a parallel universe, or the future.

We can summarize these truths as follows:

1. There are an infinite number of parallel universes.

2. Quantum waves carry information moving from past to present and from future to present.

3. We should be able to "talk" to the future as clearly as we "talk" to the past.

4. Existence as we know it is a subset of reality, which is unknowable.

The new physics relates several truths about the world, as we know it. Our lives would be meaningless without the past or the future. It is this momentary flash of consciousness containing complementary observations of an object in our reality that join together to create physical matter. This is how we can see the world as we do. If we eliminate either the past or future component, the world becomes ghostlike and nothing would exist as a solid object. In fact, our consciousness would vanish.

CHAPTER 9

Our minds are time machines, able to tune into multiple realities and sense the flow of waves from both the past and future. Existence cannot exist without this higher form of quantum reality. We are both the choosers of subsets of reality and the constructors of existence. Because we are the products of time past and time future, we are "stuck" in time.

Who Created the Past?

Did the early universe, for example, have a radius? How could it, because according to a quantum picture, it wouldn't have had any radius until that radius was measured? Who measured it? An interesting quantum truth is that it is our observation now that is determining the past.

When we observe a current event, we send a message (quantum wave) back in time and this "causes" a past event. There is no absolute past. Parallel universes come into play to explain this. The past is what a community of communicating intelligent beings choose to be the past. Other pasts are out there waiting to be discovered. In other words, there are parallel pasts - an infinite number of them. The past that is altered by the present is just one of the many.

There is no such "thing as the absolute present, according to the Theory of Relativity. What is present for someone could be the past or the future for another. Consequently, it would seem that the future also communicates with the present. This future is that which is chosen by a community of intelligent communicating persons. According to the quantum rules governing parallel worlds, there are an indefinite number of futures.

All possible futures exert an influence on the present. Since the future communicates with the present, and by the same line of reasoning, the present communicates with the past, then it must follow that time is not fixed. The truth given to us from the parallel universe theory shows that the future can influence the present just as much as the past.

Since no observer was assumed present at the beginning of time to choose the observable properties of matter, one must include the possibility that all possible parallel universes also appeared when our own universe appeared. For each and everyone of us there are parallel vous and mes somehow existing in the same space and time that we live in but normally not seen or sensed by us. Choices and decisions are being made at the exact moment in time you are choosing and deciding. The only difference is the specific outcome of your particular choice. This choice leads to a different, but similar parallel universe.

---

[1]   Fred Alan Wolf, *Taking the Quantum Leap*, Harper and Row, New York, 1981.

[2]   Fred Alan Wolf, *Parallel Universes: The Search for other Worlds*, Simon and Schuster, New York, 1988.

CHAPTER 10

MY OWN TRUTH

The Truth About Death

Death itself is not a traumatic experience. It is the birth process that is traumatic. Imagine for a moment that you are very ill and lying in a hospital bed. Then imagine your astral body lifting out and all of a sudden you are dead. It takes hours, days, or even weeks to realize that you are, in fact, dead. That is hardly traumatic. All pain and other discomforts are completely removed at the moment of death.

Now imagine yourself being born. The newborn has just acquired a subconscious and has left its cozy womb for a bright, sterile environment that is totally different and most uncomfortable compared to what it has been used to for nine months. The newborn is slapped, footprinted, suctioned, swabbed, processed, and totally dependent on strangers in white uniforms for its very survival. There is no direct data on the actual pain of the birth process, but imagine ice-cold steel forceps around your head, or a premature delivery. Personally, birth seems more intimidating to me than dying.

When we die, we are really not dead in the common use of the word. We may be nonfunctional on the earth plane but we are quite functional on other planes. We exist then on the astral plane, and eventually we will enter the white light and end up on the soul plane. So, what we think of as death is really shifting to another plane of existence.

Before I go into details about the parapsychological explanations of death, let me give you some medical facts. The cells in our body are dying and being replaced constantly. One of the purposes of the sleep state, at least from a medical point of view, is to re-create the many millions of cells that are killed during each day that we live. We are also replacing lost energy during sleep. Scientists tell us that about every nine months, each and every one of our cells has been replaced at least once. So, technically, we die every nine months. Our body is completely different from how it was one year ago and will be completely different at this time next year. We obviously don't feel dead and are able to function quite nicely. The process of cell replacement continues along so smoothly that we are not aware of anything different happening. It is our physical perception that is being fooled into thinking that the body is unchanged from year to year.

There are many types of reactions that my patients report to me when they relive a death scene in a past life regression, or a future life progression. I will discuss only the most common descriptions my patients my patients have given of the death experience.

First, a floating sensation is almost always described. Whatever physical discomforts the patient may have felt at the moment of death are completely gone. There is no pain or any other feeling at the moment. The patient is simply floating. Feelings of inner peace and quiet, with a complete absence of fear, are quite common. The body below is now viewed as if it were no longer a part of the patient. Indeed, this is exactly the case. Let me repeat, there is absolutely no danger of the patient's really dying, even in very deep trance levels, while reliving the death experience from a past life.

Patients soon realize that they have a body, but a very different type of body, subject to very different physical laws. This astral body possesses the ability to do many things that the physical body cannot. For example, this astral body can move through walls and doors and travel thousands of miles in a matter of seconds. Time is not registered at this level, and the astral body possesses complete knowledge of the former life and can even read the minds of other people who were involved in that life.

The Silver Cord

One constant Observation that people have reported to me is the presence of a pulsating "silver cord." Theoretically, when one experiences an astral projection not related to a death experience, there is a silver cord attached to the back of the head of the astral body and to the solar plexus region of the etheric body. As long as this silver cord is unbroken, the patient's physical body is still alive. Upon death, this silver cord is broken.

Death Sounds

Another observation is auditory. People hear all sorts of noises following death. Buzzing sounds that appear to originate from inside the head are commonly reported; loud ringing sounds, clicks, roars, banging noises, whistling, and musical sounds. One theory that has been proposed states that each plane has a characteristic combination of light and sound, and this will change as one ascends or descends to different planes. The individual's vibrational rate is also changing. At this time many bright colors are often seen. They change frequently and seem to move by at a very rapid rate.

The Tunnel

The feeling of moving through a long, dark tunnel is, in my opinion, the most fascinating and important observation of the death experience. Some patients use the term "vacuum." It seems as if the patient is being drawn into this tunnel, and once in this dark structure they are transported to the other side, or astral plane. This may be comparable to a time warp or a black hole.

CHAPTER 10

When I regress or progress patients, I usually suggest they imagine themselves entering a tunnel that has a bright white light at the end. I suggest that there is a fork at the end of the tunnel. If the patient takes the right fork, he or she ends up in a past life. A future life would be the destination if the left fork were taken. This technique is very successful and one of the most commonly used methods of guiding a patient into a past or future life. Whether in a hypnotic state or death, the tunnel clearly seems to represent the passageway to the next level.

The Presence of Others

Once the patient is able to stabilize him or herself after emerging from the tunnel and to adjust to the floating sensation, the presence of others is noted. By "others," I am referring to Masters and Guides who come to offer their help and guidance. Also, the patient may report seeing "dead" relatives and friends who try to help. All communication is by telepathy at this time. A feeling of warmth, security, and inner peace is usually prevalent. The patient is made to feel loved; all fears of death are removed.

The White Light

The white light (Higher Self) is the culmination of the death experience. The patient is shown the white light, which at this time will appear as an almost blinding yet peaceful aura of pure white light. This light is very similar to the image used in various healing techniques on the earth plane. By imagining that they are surrounding the damaged part of the body with this white light, patients have facilitated their own healing. On the astral plane, the patient will benefit most if he or she enters the white light, where he or she will be taken to the soul plane to reevaluate this last life and choose the next one. But, as I have mentioned before, not everyone chooses to enter the white light immediately and some may wander around the lower astral plane for many years, or even centuries, before they finally do enter.

Individual Variations

The experiences of death don't always follow the order I've described. Also, there may be time lags between each step. Some people accept the death state quickly and easily. Others require more time and guidance before they will even accept the idea of death, let alone enter the white light.

Remember, it is your expectations of what the death state is supposed to be that will affect. the actual experience. If you expect to be surrounded by haloed angels in white robes playing harps, your Masters and Guides will do their very best to create that scene for you because they know that it will make you feel comfortable. It is only when you are comfortable that these higher entities will inform you about where you are and who they are and what you are supposed to be doing.

The main point is that death is not an experience to fear. Perhaps it is not something to look forward to, but it is not to be feared.

The Experience of Death

What seems to happen at death is that you experience, it least initially, what you *expect* to experience. In other words, your expectations of what death should be like seem to affect the actual experience or perception of death. A belief in the fires of hell or the clouds of heaven will often manifest themselves, temporarily at least. Fortunately these fantasies disappear quickly and you are joined by Masters and Guides. These angel-like entities will try and help you adjust to the astral plane. They will guide you into a gradual realization that you have died and it is time to move on. You may not even accept that you have died at first, because you really won't feel much different. There is, however, one very significant difference: you are now totally free of any discomfort. Your new environment will be far less limiting than that of the physical plane, which you have just left.

On the astral plane, you may find yourself in the presence of dead relatives or friends. Telepathy is the rule now, so that your true feelings toward that friend or relative will be made known, and vice versa. There is no hypocrisy on the astral plane.

When you go to sleep every night, out-of-body experiences occur and simulate the death experience. This simulated death state is merely training for later. Dreams of flying or falling are conscious remnants of this fifth dimensional trip.

I alluded earlier to the white light. This white light is an express train to the soul plane   the plane where you will evaluate your past life and choose your next one. Your Masters and Guides and "dead" relatives and friends will advise you to enter this white light. If you do, then all is well and good. But, as I've mentioned before, if you don't, you become what is known as a "troubled spirit" and remain on the astral plane, unsure of who you are and what you are supposed to be doing. You can be observed on the earth plane as a ghost or you can be unobserved and just wander around aimlessly. You will be reminded again and again by your Masters and Guides to enter the white light. But nothing can force you to do so.

The Soul Plane

Eventually, you will enter the white light and your destination will be the soul plane. Upon arriving at the soul plane, you will be greeted by special guides who are assigned specifically to you for the purpose of orientation. Your guides will spend as much time as necessary to explain the nature of reality and discuss your present purpose on this plane. You will be shown detailed events from your last life and how they fit into your karmic patterns. Also, you will be shown scenes from past and future lives and be requested to study these events in detail.

On the soul plane, you will also be choosing your parents, brothers, sisters, and other family members, as well as planning all the major events in your life. These events must take into consideration the karmic cycle of these other people.

Not only must you be fully aware of your own karmic cycle, but you must be at least familiar with the karmic cycles of the many significant people that you will come into contact with in your new life. Whether you will be rich or poor, an only child or a member of a large family, black or white, weak or strong, will all depend on a very complicated selection process that your past life history will decide. Your Akashic records have all of this information and they will be your constant reference on the soul plane.

Akashic Records

These Akashic records are reportedly kept on the causal plane, but we do have access to them on the soul plane. They represent a file on the soul's growth and development throughout its many lives. They contain what the soul has learned and not learned. Thus, the soul's progression through its karmic cycle is what the Akashic records will show. By using these records we have intimate knowledge of what we have done and what we have to do. This is a most valuable aid.

Masters and Guides

We are aided in making these decisions by our Masters and Guides. These highly evolved entities have completed their karmic cycles and their purpose is simply to help and advise us as to our next lives. They do not moralize or pass judgment. They simply counsel us and try to help us as best they can. The individual soul always has free will to ignore their advice. Many of our decisions are poorly made for this very reason. These Masters and Guides also receive advice from even higher entities with higher vibrational rates in the seven higher planes. These much more advanced entities receive their advice from even more evolved sources, the ultimate authority being God. The final result is, of course, excellent guidance. When we listen to these guides, we make better decisions and work out our karmic cycles faster and with much less trauma.

Choosing a New Body

In choosing your next life, the earth plane may not be to your liking. In that case you might choose any of the other lower planes (astral, causal, mental or etheric) to work out your karmic cycle. Life on these other planes isn't very different from that on the earth plane. People get married, have children, divorce, love, hate, etc. on all of the lower planes. However, beyond the earth plane there is simultaneous time.

This is a very complicated process and group karmic considerations must be met. That is, you have to consider the karmic cycle of dozens of other entities before you can finalize your plans. These other entities must agree with your plans because they also have free will. This veto power can cause untold delays in the final framework of your and their next lives.

There can even be competition for certain bodies. Let's assume that you have completed your design of the basic framework for your next life. Now you must choose a newborn to enter. But let's say that another entity desires this same newborn for his or her karmic cycle and gets the right to inhabit it. You still have a karmic cycle to work out with the parents and other members of that newborn's family. You will now have to find another suitable newborn and devise a way to relate karmically to the parents and other family members of the newborn you were prevented from entering. We don't know exactly how the order on the waiting list for bodies is decided. It is probably based on a priority system giving those souls with the most important karmic lessons to learn first priority.

Once you have carefully chosen your next body and designed the basic framework of your next life, you are ready for the soul's entrance into the newborn. During the course of the pregnancy, each soul may visit its future body. Indeed, many souls actually enter the developing fetus, and this is why many people have prenatal memories that can be tapped through the use of hypnosis.

The soul or subconscious actually enters the body of the new born within 24 hours before or after the birth of the child. Many times during our childhood the soul will leave the body. This will occur during the waking hours as well as at night as the entity sleeps. All throughout our life the soul will leave the body during our sleep state, because it is during this sleep state that our Masters and Guides can continue teaching and advising us on our earthly progress. Thus, we are never really without the benefit of our guides, and the process of learning that began in between our lives never really ends.

Other Decisions on the Soul Plane

Much counsel is given to an entity on the soul plane. However, even with all this advice and plenty of time to make these decisions, some people choose to reincarnate before they are advised to. This is unfortunate because the necessary planning has not occurred. Instead of saving time, much time will be wasted and many errors will be made.

Relationships represent important decisions on the soul plane. Telepathic communication between you and the other entities involved will establish the details of who you will relate with and how in your next life. Your son in this life may be your father in your next life. Your wife or husband may be your brother or employer or parent.

Light People

Every so often I regress patients only to find that they are not in a physical form. They do not possess a body. They are pure energy. The most common form of energy is light. The term "light people" has been used to describe entities that do not take physical form. Sasha's case is actually quite typical of a "light people" regression.

Sasha had experienced some unusual dreams of swirling light accompanied by an intense feeling of being controlled. This is an indicator of a "light people" past life regression.

These regressions are, by far, the most difficult to conduct. The patient appears to be struggling to communicate and is censored from an outside source. During Sasha's regression, she described herself as being of pure light. She informed me that her "source" was green.

Sasha lived in another galaxy many light years from the Earth. Her position in that society was to monitor the selection of her people who were to travel to less evolved planets for the purpose of scientific study.

She was particularly stressed about her work. Sasha felt very insecure concerning her ability to properly evaluate her fellow light sources for their respective assignments.

As I progressed her forward, she revealed to me that many errors were made due to her negligence. This resulted in quite a few problems with these assignments. My questioning was interrupted several times by Sasha's supervisor who would not allow her to communicate with me.

After much effort I was able to determine that Sasha was being severely disciplined for her negligence. She was placed in a type of "room" during this trial. I use the term room to describe this place, but it was more of a fifth dimensional magnetic field.

This room contained various pulsating light forms (Sasha's superiors and judges), as well as voids through which these pulsating light forms could come and go as they pleased.

Sasha was confined to a type of force field during her trial. The result of her case was that she was judged to be grossly incompetent. As punishment her source was demoted to yellow and she was to be banished from her planet.

Since many of her errors involved the planet Earth, these judges sentenced her to be trapped in a human body and become a part of what we term today as the karmic cycle.

During the latter stages of this regression, it again became increasingly difficult to obtain any information. Sasha was being censored. The words came out slowly and only with great difficulty.

Usually, these "light people" explore their first incarnation on Earth, and represent about five percent of past life regressions I conduct. Most patients who have these types of experiences show very little interest in extraterrestrial life, as was the case with Sasha. They usually seek my services for habit elimination or some other problem.

UFOs and PSI Phenomena

There are MANY reports of UFOs by police officers, pilots, air traffic controllers, meteorologists - trained observers. And, reports which can not be explained away as plasma, ball lightning, Venus or swamp gas. Actually, they all can be explained, away, by a disingenuous mind, or someone in denial as to UFO reality.

The Parapsychological Association, an international scientific society, was elected an affiliate of the American Association for the Advancement of Science (AAAS) in 1969. Seminars on psi research have formed part of the regular programs of annual conferences of the American Association for the Advancement of Science, the American Psychological Association, and the American Statistical Association. Educated audiences at the United Nations, Harvard, and Bell Laboratories have invited lecturers on the state of psi research. Reports have been prepared by the Congressional Research Service, the Army Research Institute, the National Research Council, the Office of Technology Assessment, and the American Institutes for Research (this latter one commissioned by the CIA). All five of the reviews concluded that, based on experimental evidence, certain forms of psychic phenomena deserved serious scientific study.

CHAPTER 10

Progression

In 1977 I asked a patient, while she was in a hypnotic trance, to go to the origin of her problem. It was my expectation that she would regress back to. a prior life. Instead, she described a future life in the twenty-third century. This was the birth of progression hypnotherapy. My first book, *Past Lives - Future Lives* (originally published in 1982) was the first book ever written documenting this phenomenon.

The actual experience of a progression is rather difficult to describe. I have personally conducted thousands of progressions. Most people are afraid of the future and don't want to be progressed. Also, I have regressed myself into past lives and progressed myself into future lives, so that I can speak of these phenomena from personal experience. In a regression, the scenes can unfold in a logical and orderly fashion. The patient can recall the past in great detail, and these journeys into the past are often quite helpful to the patient in terms of understanding present karma and current behavior problems.

A progression, however, is far less stable. It is much more difficult to obtain information. When I perform progressions, I am essentially attempting to see how a patient's karma will be manifested in the future. This knowledge can be very helpful to a patient in terms of the present.

It seems that when an individual is progressed into the future, he or she may be quickly removed from a particular scene and transferred to another without any instructions or cues from me. These sudden dislocations pose absolutely no anger to the patient, of course, but the continuity of the experience may be lost or fractured. For example, the patient could be describing a scene in some futuristic city. The next thing we know, the city has disappeared and a desert scene has replaced it. The patient may then describe a third and completely different scene, and act as if nothing unusual has happened.

The concept of "forbidden knowledge" is often mentioned by my patients. People ask me, "isn't knowledge of future events prohibited by the universe?" The answer is simple. If you are supposed to know something, such as your future, your Higher Self will see to it that you receive that data. If, however, you are not supposed to be aware of certain future events, then no person, place or thing will give you that information (unless and until you are ready to receive it). Even with my highly sophisticated techniques and extraordinary success rates, I cannot arrange for you to receive information that you are supposed to have. When the student is ready, the teacher will be there.

The Principle of Forgiveness

What is interesting to note about working out our karma is the principle of forgiveness. When I have the patient speak from the superconscious (the highest level of the subconscious) mind level, I am informed of how this principle works. Assume that you lived during the time of the Vikings, about 1,200 years ago. Raiding villages, burning buildings, raping the women, and murdering the villagers would have been commonplace. This would incur much negative karma. If during one of these raids a certain group of villagers would have their lives spared because of your kindness, then you would have earned positive karma. It wouldn't be just one positive episode against many negative ones. The fact that you showed this kindness would erase many negative episodes during that particular incarnation. If you spent the rest of that life helping other people, all of the past murders, thefts, and other crimes could be removed from your karmic cycle.

Free Will

Since the soul always has free will, it is our decision to be born at a certain time and place. It is our decision to choose our parents, friends, lovers and enemies. We cannot blame other people or a bad childhood or marriage for our present problems. We are directly responsible for our lives because we have chosen the environment. The basic framework of your new life will be preplanned by you, but you cannot plan every situation. Not only does your soul have free will, but so do all the souls that you will come into contact with in this new life. The main point is that you choose the tests.

Group Karma

We do not reincarnate individually. Rather, as I have been suggesting, our own separate karmic cycles are intertwined with many others. For example, your parents may have been your children in a former life. Your wife may have been your brother or son, etc. This is not to say that karma involves any form of incest or other such moral judgment. It simply implies that our lessons are intermingled with the lessons of their entities. These lessons have an effect between entities and among others around them.

Scientific Evidence for a Soul

What is actually traveling through the fifth dimension is our soul occupying a spiritual body, This is the astral body in the astral plane, causal body in the causal plane, and so on. So let us discuss actual evidence for the existence of the soul.

First, we must establish the fact that the soul is electromagnetic radiation, equivalent to a radio or television signal. Most of this harmless radiation in our physical universe is electromagnetic radiation. Second, the individual entering the fifth dimension via their soul contacts a reality outside of them self. Some refer to this as consciousness.

Dr. William Tiller, professor emeritus at Stanford University in the Department of Materials Science and Engineering, has demonstrated that human consciousness (the soul or subconscious mind) contributes to the creation and direction of the universe. His research involves the use of intention imprinted electrical devices (IIEDs) to illustrate how human intention can influence physical reality with measurement amplitude changes to water, enzymes, fruit fly larvae, etc. by as much as 100 times the instrument measurement accuracy. In other words, Tiller showed how our soul significantly altered the properties of physical materials.[1]

The neuroscientist Mario Beauregard showed that life-changing spiritual events can be documented. He demonstrated that religious experiences have a nonmaterial origin.[2]

Scientific materialism is at a loss to explain irrefutable accounts of mind over matter, of intuition, willpower, and leaps of faith, of the "placebo effect" in medicine, of near-death experiences on the operating table, and of psychic premonitions of a loved one in crisis, to say nothing of the occasional sense of oneness with nature and mystical experiences in meditation or prayer.

Subtle energy refers to the medium through which consciousness acts on the realm of matter and energy. This subtle energy appears to contribute to many phenomena not currently explained by conventional science: telekinesis, remote sensing, telepathy, intuition, healing by prayer or other psychic means, biocommunication between species, etc. Since these phenomena have tangible effects that can be documented but not explained by the known principles of the electromagnetic field of matter/energy, they require that we hypothesize another force through which conscious intent acts on the affected objects, senses and cells.

Subtle energy communication happens only when behaviors, thoughts or talk are based in emotions or serious intent. Words or ideas per se do not elicit a reaction unless that have been energized by some force, such as subtle energy. Tests done with a distance of over three hundred miles between a donor of white cells and the lab indicates the communication bond is not affected by distance. Experiments with leukocytes (white cells) indicated that a bond of communication exists between an individual's thoughts/emotions and his cells after they are removed from the donor's body. The existence of interspecies communication as this level demonstrates the singular and, apparently, universal nature of consciousness.

We know that the brain mediates, but does not produce spiritual experiences. There is no scientific evidence showing that delusions or hallucinations can induce the long-term positive transformation that frequently follows spiritual experiences. Most delusions and hallucinations result in negative encounters. Spiritual experiences are not the outcome of particular genes or neural disorders, nor can they be created merely by the use of technology.

The God Gene

Molecular biologist Dean Hamer, chief of gene structure at the U.S. National Cancer Institute, proposed the existence of a "God Gene." He states that a gene known as VMAT2 (vesicular monoamine transporter) is the God gene. We know that the brain's temporal lobes and the limbic system are involved in spiritual/mystical experiences. This does not mean that these areas create the experiences all by themselves.

Spiritual experiences are neurally instantiated by different brain regions involved in a variety of functions, such as self-consciousness, emotion, body representation, visual and motor imagery, and spiritual perception. These phenomena are complex and multidimensional. Upon dissection of the human brain, aside from some jelly-type matter, nerve fibers and perhaps neurotransmitters, all of which come into play in our thought and functions, there emerges not a shred of evidence of a substance that produces a sense of humor, the appreciation of art, or the ability to differentiate between good and evil.

Dr. Michael Persinger, a neuropsychologist at Laurentian University in Sudbury, Ontario, has invented a helmet (called the Octopus or God Helmet) that allegedly induces spiritual/mystical experiences by electromagnetically stimulating the temporal lobes of those who wear it. This God Helmet is actually a snowmobile helmet with solenoids that purportedly could stimulate subjects to experience God.

Persinger's research failed to demonstrate any consistency in his reported God Helmet experiences. He offers no imaging data to support his claims about what is happening in subject's brains; rather, he relies on inference from the subjective reports of his subjects.

Persinger was routinely turned down for Natural Sciences and Engineering Research Council of Canada (NSERC) grants. He was reported to finance most of his research in this area himself, through his work as a clinical psychologist. In a highly secular country like Canada, the fact that Persinger's research might discomfit the religious is not a likely reason for NSERC's lack of interest. Persinger's specific claim is that such experiences can be reliably triggered by electromagnetic waves directed at the temporal lobes has failed to pass any scientific test.

We now know that there are several brain regions, not just the temporal lobes, are involved in mystical experiences. These include the inferior parietal lobule, visual cortex, caudate nucleus, and left brain stem as well as many other areas. There is no single "God spot" in the brain located in the temporal lobes.

Universal Laws

Although there are dozens of universal laws, I will summarize what I feel are the most important ones. Since these universal laws (truths) represent the main difference between religion and spirituality, let us discuss them:

1. **The Law of Free Will.** Since the soul always has free will, it is our decision to be born at a certain time and place. It is our decision to choose our parents, mends, lovers, and enemies. We cannot blame other people or a bad childhood or marriage for our present problems. We are directly responsible for our lives because we have chosen the environment. The basic framework of your new life will be preplanned by you, but you can't plan every situation. Not only does your soul have free will, but so do all the souls that you will come into contact with in this new life. The main point there is that you choose the tests.

Although many of the major events in your life are laid out by you on the soul plane prior to your birth, you have free will to sidestep your destiny. Also, you always have free will in how you respond to any situation. If you respond with love, compassion and integrity, you have probably learned your karmic lesson and will not have to repeat the experience in the future. We alone have the power to choose good over evil and growth over stagnation or degeneration. Only you can facilitate your spiritual growth and perfect your soul. Never blame any person, place or thing for your lot in life. It is free will that caused our fall from grace originally.

2. **The Law of Grace.** Karma can be experienced to the letter of the law or in mercy and grace. Wisdom erases karma. If you show mercy, grace and love, you will receive the same in return. This is also known as the principle of forgiveness. If you eliminate a negative behavior or weakness now, you erase all previous karma debts and don't have to work out any past life carryovers with every individual you may have wronged in the past, or who may have hurt you in previous existences.

3. **The Law of Challenge.** The universe never presents us with opportunities we cannot handle. You may be emotionally or physically overwhelmed, but not spiritually. Each obstacle and reward is place in our path to both challenge us and facilitate our growth as a soul.

4. **The Law of Karma.** This law focuses on cause and effect. For every action there is a reaction. Nothing happens by mere chance. We select the framework, including all obstacles and rewards, on the soul plane prior to our birth. Since we choose' all of these lessons, there is nobody else to blame for our circumstances. "To thine own self be true."

194

5. All of our actions, particularly our motives, have consequences. If you follow universal laws you will perfect the soul and ascend, as wisdom erases karma. If you continue repeating mistakes and fail lessons (you choose those lessons on the soul plane), you are asking for a long and frustrating karmic cycle of many dysfunctional lives.

6. **The Law of Attraction.** Like attracts like. Whatever you focus your energy on you will attract. If you are negative, you draw in and experience negativity. If you are loving, you draw in and experience love.

7. **The Law of Resistance.** You tend to attract those individuals and karmic lessons which you have resisted. This is a "mirror of karma" law.

8. **The Law of Divine Flow.** By accessing our Higher Self (superconscious mind), we are functioning as a channel for the God energy complex and can accelerate our spiritual growth at a rapid rate. This law also explains how miracles occur.

9. **The Law of Polarity.** Everything has an opposite on the physical plane. These opposites (left, right, up, down, love, fear, good, evil, hot, cold, etc.) are identical in composition but only differ in direction or degree. This law is the foundation for the dual aspects of our world.

10. **The Law of Reciprocity.** The more you give, the more you will receive. The more you assist others, the more you assist yourself.

11. **The Law of Manifestation.** Our mind, not our brain, creates the material world we live. Quantum physics

demonstrates how this mechanism works mathematically. Be careful for what you desire - it may very well come true.

12. **The Law of Consciousness.** Our consciousness (soul) is constantly expanding and thereby creating more opportunities for our spiritual growth. We can also lengthen our karmic cycle if we fail to follow universal laws.

13. **The Law of Abundance.** It is our mind (consciousness) that creates abundance. Through self-hypnosis and visualization techniques we can attract money, relationships, fame, better communication, spirituality and other goals into our reality.

14. **The Law of Correspondence.** This principle deals with what is known as the "mirror of karma." "As above so below" also applies here. The outer world (macrocosm) we live in is a reflection of the inner world (microcosm) of our consciousness. All objects created on the physical plane have a counterpart on the Astral plane. This law helps to establish an interconnectedness between all components of our universe.

15. **The Law of the Present Moment.** We live in a space-time continuum in which the past, present and future occurs simultaneously. It is only within our mind that we limit ourselves to the concepts of linear time. In reality, all that exists is in the present moment. In the higher planes, where all souls are perfect, this is referred to as the "Eternal Now."

16. **The Law of Cycles.** As we discussed with the law of polarity, our universe is characterized by cycles. Day becomes night, winter ends and spring begins and whatever rises, eventually falls and rises again. This principle helps explain how our universe began (big bang) and will

eventually collapse and rise again in a 40-billion year cyclic pattern.

17. **The Law of Reincarnation.** This law is also known as the wheel of reincarnation or law of cyclic return. As long as we have lessons to learn (karma), our soul will be required to reincarnate into a body. It is only when perfection of the soul is achieved that this seemingly endless cycle is terminated and our soul merges with our Higher Self to ascend into the higher planes to reunite with God.

Summarizing Universal Laws

- We contain the power and energy of God in the form of our Higher Self. Unless we allow someone power over us, no other person can truly determine our destiny.

- We create our own reality through our thoughts, desires, feelings, attitudes, fears, beliefs, expectations and actions. Our world can and will change when we alter our thinking.

- We all contain the capability in the present moment to change any limiting beliefs and custom design our destiny. No past experience or perceived .future can limit our spiritual growth unless we allow it to.

- The energy of the universe moves in the direction we select. Positive outlooks result in empowered futures, and cynical attitudes manifest as unnecessary struggles.

- The universe and all humans exist foremost because of love. When we acknowledge this principle we are both happy and moving closer to our eventual ascension.

- There is no absolute or ultimate truth. Truth lies in our own consciousness and level of spiritual evolvement.

---

1   William Tiller, *Conscious Acts of Creation*, Pavior Publishers, Walnut Creek, CA 2001.

2   Mario Beauregard and Denyse O'Leary, *The Spiritual Brain: A Neuroscientist's Case for the Existence of the Soul*, Harper Collins, NY, 2008.

CHAPTER 11

THE ULTIMATE TRUTH

One truth I have noted throughout this incarnation is that nothing worthwhile is easy. Deciphering the Ultimate Truth is a most worthwhile endeavor. It has resulted in man traveling all over the world to seek this truth. Whether it be the Himalayas in Tibet, or the Andes in South America, or a Native American shaman, we have used this external approach to seek the Ultimate Truth.

What is the secret of life? Is there life after death? What is beyond the farthest point in the universe? Does life exist on other planets? Was there an Atlantis and Lemuria? Is there a God? These and many other questions make up components to the Ultimate Truth. You may, indeed, have your own to add to this list.

There are some people who read the end of a novel first, perhaps, to avoid the. tension of a shocking climax to the story. If you are one of these readers and have turned to this chapter first, please return to chapter one and read this book as it was written. You will not appreciate what I am about to say otherwise.

For those of you who have patiently read this book in sequence, I will now discuss the Ultimate Truth. Let me begin with an all important truth. The direction of this pure truth is inward, never outward. For those of you who have traveled the four corners and seven seas of our planet, I applaud your persistence. However, you could not possibly have found the Ultimate Truth.

For one thing, if you did, you most certainly would not be reading this book. I would be reading yours. Secondly, all of the "gurus" and mentors in the world cannot give you this desired piece of knowledge. As I mentioned before, the direction one needs to go to find the Ultimate Truth is within oneself. Shakespeare said, "To thine own self be true." Throughout this book, you will note certain common themes. Think of it as the ultimate empowerment or karmic identity. Whether it be Zen's One-ness of "cosmic consciousness," or the superconscious, the answer lies with ourselves.

Cayce, Seth, quantum physics, theosophy, ECK, the mystery schools, the Sufis, Plato and on and on, all taught this truth. Some emphasize dreams as a means of accessing our higher selves. Others suggest reading the Akashic records. Still others promote various alpha techniques (hypnosis, meditation, astral travel, yoga, etc.) to facilitate this important truth.

Many of these approaches allude to the psychic powers that are characteristic of those who grow spiritually and become a Master. Others discuss ascending to the higher planes and being with God (the Absolute, the Infinite, the One, All That Is, the Source, etc.) in heaven or Nirvana or the God plane.

Most describe an in-between life state and refer to it as purgatory, bardo or the soul plane. Just about all of these professors of truth describe a mechanism of reincarnation, with appropriate references to some form of karmic reward and punishment.

The idea of a simultaneous time concept is an important component of the truths of the new physics, Seth and the Eastern philosophies. Even the existentialists emphasize the meaninglessness of life without some form of truth regarding God and the past and future.

Most of these sources focus in on our responsibilities for our own growth and the consequences of our actions. "Whatsoever a man soweth, that shall he also reap." "What goes around comes around."

Whether it be in a parallel universe, a future life, a resurrected body in purgatory or beyond space-time, they seem to be implying something beyond this life.

The only way you, as a seeker of the Ultimate Truth, are going to resolve this, is to look inwardly. You may pick and choose from the above menu of metaphysical options but it is still your responsibility to do your homework. No one human being or any external source can give you the answer to this question, what is the Ultimate Truth?

I do not mean to frustrate or tease you with this book's theme. As in the Mystery School's philosophy of training initiates to acquire secrets of the universe, you are both the initiate and the Master (at least potentially). You are a Buddha waiting to blossom as a flower does in the spring or a caterpillar evolving into a butterfly.

No book or guru can empower you. Only you can empower yourself. Discovering the ultimate truth is one form of empowerment that is unequaled by anything you have ever experienced. It is your destiny, not fate. It is your light at the end of the tunnel.

There appears to be three main schools of metaphysical thought concerning the quest for the Ultimate Truth. We have discussed various mental theories, fostered by those partial to an intellectual approach. Secondly, there is the school of cosmic consciousness. Lastly, the various approaches of out-of-body experiences and fifth dimensional travel have been described. Each of these approaches, naturally, feel they have discovered the Ultimate Truth.

Most saints and holy men talk about leaving their physical bodies at will and transcending to higher planes, where they receive their ultimate truths. In fact, one who is competent to give a man this personal experience of withdrawal or temporary separation from the body and who can, thus, put him on the way to higher spiritual realms, is a genuine master, saint, or sat guru.

One principle that is commonly taught in other systems' truth, is that of love. It is more than loving one's enemies as much as we love ourselves. It is a lifestyle of truly practicing love each and every day in everything that we do. It is a Vulcan mind meld approach to New Age principles that have been around since man has occupied this planet.

There are some behavior that we as living beings can do to facilitate our spiritual growth and the attainment of the Ultimate Truth. These ways of spiritual living may be summarized as follows.

1. Be loving, unselfish and kind. Love is the most important quality in the universe.

2. Be a giver. Eliminate the tendency to take from others. Live a more simple and quality life.

3. Decrease the attachment to material possessions. Enjoy them all you want but be willing to lose them without envy, resentment, anger and other negative emotional responses.

4. Be empowered. You may want certain things out of life, but never be needy.

5. Be God-oriented instead of world-oriented.

6. Be humble. Eliminate the desire to be ruthless, aggressive and conceited. Remove all tendencies to be superficial, vain and phony.

7. Learn not to identify too strongly with our body. Say to yourself, "I am a spiritual soul, immortal and eternal. I create my own reality." The body eventually dies, but the soul is eternal.

With technological advancement, there is a trend toward depersonalization in our world. Our lives seem to be numbered, stamped, and processed without a human mind to mediate the action. But self-identification is still within us all. By exploring the fifth dimension through our subconscious, we can find out who we really are and what makes us tick. It is when we reach our threshold of tolerance of the processed world around us that we rebel with violence, hatred, and fear. By looking within ourselves, we can improve our individual lives and the quality of society as a whole. As a result, we can have an optimistic vision of our collective future.

We have a choice. The soul always has free will. We can choose to do good or evil, right or wrong. We choose our future lives. Who would choose to kill, rape, steal, or cheat if he or she realized the karmic implications? By learning to use these principles of karma to better ourselves, we are bettering the future for us all.

Many people ask me to help them speed up their karmic cycles so that they won't have to come back again. I can't do that. Only you can do that. Be honest, truthful, and faithful to your own code of ethics. If you follow; this simple advice, you are well on your way to the higher planes.

This entire process will and when you fulfill your karma. When you learn all the lessons you have to learn and show kindness and unselfish love to all those with whom you come into contact, the cycle will end. When it ends, you will go beyond the soul plane to the higher planes and, eventually, to God. Karma is merely a process of evolution, of achieving greater levels of perfection. It opens the door to our Ultimate Truth.

Learn to love oneself and others. Learn to love God, whatever that means to you. Access your own Higher Self, and you will find the Ultimate Truth. Your Ultimate Truth will be different than mine. It will not be similar to anyone else's. Just as another person's denture wouldn't fit you (as a retired dentist, I can use metaphors such as this), neither would their Ultimate Truth.

To find your Ultimate Truth, I suggest some type of alpha technique. It may be hypnosis (by far the most efficient), meditation, yoga, or anything that relaxes you, and allows you to enter an altered state of consciousness.

CHAPTER 11

There are no absolute truths, including what I just said. Einstein showed us in his truth that everything is relative. There is an Ultimate Truth, but only the inner you can inform you of it. Only your true consciousness, your superconscious, can share with you the Ultimate Truth; the light at the end of the tunnel.

BIBLIOGRAPHY

Beauregard, M. and O'Leary, D. *The Spiritual Brain: A Neuroscientist's Case for the Existence of the Soul*. New York: Harper Collins, 2008.

Brandon, S. F. *History. Time and Deity*. New York: Barnes and Noble, 1965.

Crookall, R. *The Study and Practice of Astral Projection*. London: Aquarian Press, 1961.

Darwin, C. *Origin of Species*. Buffalo: Prometheus Books, 1991.

Eliade, M. *Cosmos and History: The Myth of the Eternal Return*. New York: Harper & Row, 1959.

Goldberg, Bruce. *Past Lives-Future Lives*. New York: Ballantine Books, 1988.

---. *Spirit Guide Contact Through Hypnosis*. Franklin Lakes, NJ: New Age Books, 2005.

---. *Astral Voyages*. St. Paul, MN: Llewellyn Pub., 1999.

---. *Time Travelers From Our Future: A Fifth Dimension Odyssey*. Woodland Hills, CA: BG, Inc., 1999.

---. *Egypt: An Extraterrestrial and Time Traveler Experiment*. Woodland Hills, CA: BG, Inc., 2002.

---. *The Search for Grace: A Documented Case of Murder and Reincarnation. Sedona, AZ: In Print Pub., 1994.*.

---. *Ascension: The Art of Soul Perfection and the Attainment of Grace*. Woodland Hills, CA: BG, Inc., 2009.

---. *Past Lives, Future Lives Revealed*. Franklin Lakes, NJ: New Age Books, 2004.

---. *Custom Design Your Own Destiny*. Woodland Hills, CA: BG, Inc., 2007.

---. "Quantum Physics and its application to past life regression and future life progression hypnotherapy." *Journal of Regression Therapy*, 1993, 7 (1), 89-93.

---. "The clinical use of hypnotic regression and progression in hypnotherapy." *Psychology - A Journal of Human Behavior*, 1990, 27 (1), 43-48.

---. "Your problem may come from your future: a case study." *Journal of Regression Therapy*, 1990, 4 (2), 21-29.

Head, J. and Cranston, J. L. *Reincarnation: An East-West Anthology*. Wheaton, IL: The Theosophical Pub. House, 1961.

James, W. *The Principles of Psychology*. New York: Henry Holt, 1890.

Koestenbaum, P. "The vitality of death." *The Journal of Existentialism*, 1964, 5, 141.

Moody, R. A. *Life After Life*. New York: Bantam Books, 1975.

The Light Beyond. New York: Bantam Books, 1988.

Nhat Hanh, Thich. *Old Path, White Clouds*. Berkeley, CA: Parallax Press, 1991.

Osis, K. and Haroldsson, E. *At the Hour of Death*. New York: Avon, 1977.

Plato. *The Republic* (trans. Richard W. Sterling). New York: Norton, 1996.

Ring, K. *Life at Death*. New York: Coward, Mc Cann & Geoghegan, 1980.

Sabom, M. *Recollections of Death: A Medical Investigation*. New York: Harper & Row, 1982.

St. Augustine. *Confessions* (trans. Vernon J. Bourke). New York: Fathers of the Church, Inc., 1953.

Tiller, W. *Conscious Acts of Creation*. Walnut Creek, CA: Pavier Publishers, 2001.

Wolf, F. A. *Taking the Quantum Leap*. New York: Harper & Row, 1981.

---. *Parallel Universes: The Search for Other Worlds*. New York: Simon and Schuster, 1988.

Lightning Source UK Ltd.
Milton Keynes UK
07 December 2009

147150UK00002B/2/P

9 781579 681210